THURS.
5 – 5:45
6 – 6:45
7 – 7:45

Street Smart

The Handbook on Drug and Alcohol Abuse

SECOND PRINTING

By
Dr. R. L. Wright
Retired From Undercover Narcotics / Federal
Drunk Driving Unit
And
Joshua Wright
Recovering Drug Addict

Street Smart

Dr. R. L. Wright
And
Joshua A. Wright

Published By
Brentwood Christian Press
4000 Beallwood Avenue
Columbus, Georgia 31904

This Book Is Dedicated To My First Grandson

Logan Abram Wright
Born On January 4th 2004

Dr. R. L. Wright
Joshua A. Wright

Table of Contents

Chapter One
A Cop's View

A Cop's Story

If I could paint a picture of Baltimore, what would I paint? Would it be a quiet sunset sinking ever so slowly behind City Hall? Or a gentle snow blowing past the street lights in Patterson Park? Maybe a painting of innocent children playing in the streets during a summer rain, cooling themselves off on one of Baltimore's hot summer days.

These painting would all be appealing to the eye; but I couldn't paint pictures like that. Why? Because my eyes can't see beyond the blood filled alleyways, or the lifeless bodies that line the halls of the medical examiner office. I could not paint a peaceful picture of Baltimore, because of the screams for help that came from innocent victims that seem to still echo on every street corner and alleyway that we walk down; and having no idea of what happen there the night before.

If I were to paint this picture, what colors would I use? Well... I would use the colors of our flag, red, white, and blue and then add a touch of black to finish this macabre picture that has embraced my soul from the very first day I started working as a cop in the big city.

I would need lots of RED so I could show the blood of victims that flowed freely down the streets and alleyways of this once peaceful metropolis. I would also need RED to show the ambulance rushing about the city streets carrying away victims of shootings and stabbings to the local hospitals, in hopes that a life could be saved. I would use the RED to show fire trucks rushing to a vacant house that was set on fire by some a crack head that was high on his dope.

I would need lots of WHITE to show the heroin and cocaine that is being sold to our kids in the schools and on the street corners of this decaying city, that is filled with the stench of the maggots that live off the already dead but not buried drug users.

I would need BLUE to show the police officers that try to protect a society that is filled with people that are living in a hell-ish nightmare and will never wake up.

And to finish my painting, I would need black to show the hearse carrying away innocent people who lost their lives at such a young age in a city that could not protect from the devilry of a society that has no appreciation for human life.

The stories you are about to read are all true. I was a cop, I was there and you will now take a short walk with me through the savage streets of Baltimore. I will share with you the memories of the inhumane treatment that people are capable of inflicting upon each other because of drugs, greed and turf.

Street Smart is a book that will open your eyes to the world of drugs and alcohol abuse. You will be educated as to just what can happen to a person who decides to live his or her life in a world of drugs. So if you're going to use drugs know what you're getting into. Because you will meet some of the most sadistic people that have ever walked on the face of this earth. The drug dealer is not your friend, he or she is a disease that will grow on you like a cancer that invades the body. And when it's all over you will have destroyed your life and the lives of every person around you. And if you try to escape, kicking the drug habit will be the biggest battle of your life. If you can't escape then...most likely you will die and leave that little girl or little boy behind who calls you daddy or mommy.

The Price You Pay

Someone has just introduced you to marijuana and you took a hit. The first hit is always free, but you will pay for it for the rest of your life if you continue to use. So think about what your doing and why your doing it. If your friend gave you the marijuana, then he or she is not your friend.

Did you know that marijuana is a non-motivating drug? And did you know that most heroin addicts would tell you that they started out smoking marijuana? That's right! They tried it just like your trying it; and they fell in love with it. It's like dating; first you meet then before you know it your getting married. Marijuana is just a date. Soon you could be married to the real love of your life, HEROIN or COCAINE.

People will say that marijuana will calm you down. The funny thing is that you will be so clam that you may not want to go to work or to school. Then, before you know it your taking you're hard earned savings and buying marijuana every week. Following that you sell your favorite tapes and other personal things you have always cherished over the years just so you can have your bag of weed. Well Guess what? If your doing that now it won't be long until you will start to see things in a different set of eyes. Soon you will have new friends. They will be more sinister than your old companions, and their outlook on life is lived hour by hour, day by day. The only dreams they chase is the dream of a more intense high.

As your relationship with drugs grows, the need for money will also grow. The more drugs you use the more money you need. You will become a beggar, a thief, and a liar.

Your appearance will be like a prisoner of war, your body will become gaunt and your facial features will remind your loved ones of the picture found on a poison bottle. You will rip the hearts out of your parents like a skilled surgeon; you will hang your head in shame and will not be able to look friends and family members in the eye.

Your depression will flow over to the ones that love you and your promises of stopping will fall to deaf ears.

If that is not enough, soon you will start counting the friends that have died on the streets after they overdose, some who fired rat poison into their vain thinking all along it was the heroin they just bought in the roach infested vacant house down the street. And that new leather coat your girlfriend got you for Christmas…give it time and you will sell it just like you did everything else that you owned, just for that fix of heroin or cocaine.

Adding to this appalling profile of a once good-looking person I must ask this question, have you ever seen the movie *"The Waking Dead"*? Well that's what people look like soon after their addiction to heroin or cocaine. And just when you thought things couldn't get any worse, the addiction to these drugs could cause you to become a streetwalker, better know in police terms as a prostitute. These prostitutes are both male and female and they perform sex acts for just enough money to pay for there next fix.

Why prostitution you ask? It's simple; the addicted person cannot hold a job. They can't get money from friends because all of their friends are addicted too. And the family at some point will stop giving. The end result will be to get the money the easiest way they can, and prostitution is a trade that has been around for a long time.

Buyer Beware

The person buying the drugs off the street from a drug dealer has no idea what they are really buying. With heroin you never know what you're getting. Heroin is cut down, in other words you never get 100% pure heroin. So most of the time the buyer has no idea just how strong the product is when the purchase is made.

A buyer may get heroin that is strong one time and the next time he buys the heroin it may be weak. This is the reason some heroin users die from overdosing. It's like playing Russian roulette.

A drug dealer will live off of the misery of the drug user. The fact is the user becomes an inessential part of the drug game. The dealers could care less who lives or who dies.

A smart drug dealer will never use his product, he will only sell. But what does he sell? I recall finding a young man in an alley just off Eastern Ave. He was only seventeen and he died from an overdose, not an overdose of heroin but of rat poison. When I found him, he still had the needle still in his arm. He had foam coming from his mouth and nose. His eyes were rolled back in his head. His frozen facial expression told me that he died a horrible death.

Drug users have told me countless times of situations where they were ripped off by the drug dealers. Thinking they were buying one thing and getting something else. Think about it; you rob, steal and con people out of their money to get money for your next fix. Then you get ripped by the man who sells you white powder that looks like heroin but its really some other *#@!* that wouldn't get a rat high. So you go out and rob, steal, and con more people and try it all over again, but this time you go to a new location.

Ask any drug user and they will tell you stories of other drug users robbing them at gun point. Other users will tell you how they have been beat up and robbed as they traveled through drug infested neighborhoods making their pilgrimage to the dealer's location. And if they make it to their destination unmolested then they must travel back to their haven of rest, dreaming as they go of the high that will soon inundate their pathetic bodies.

What many users don't understand is that drug dealers don't play games. If you cross a drug dealer the repercussions can be catastrophic. Not only will they kill you, they have been know to kill entire families. In Baltimore, an entire family was killed because parents stood up to a drug dealer. Our society has become weak-kneed when it comes to standing up atrocities of the unmerciful drug dealer.

I know of a young man whose life was taken by a drug dealer. His death appeared to be an overdose and it was. However, the heroin the young man pushed into his veins was of such great quality that it took his life immediately. Any dealer can terminate a life by providing a higher grade of heroin to the user; this has been know to happen if a drug dealer has been crossed by the user or thinks the user has become a police informant. And when the user fires up the heroin he dies; and the drug dealer gets away with murder. And sadly the soul of the insignificant drug user passes on to a better place; leaving behind his tormented life and a grieving family.

Because of The High

After all the resources for money have been exhausted; the frangible life of the drug user declines even more. They no longer care about how they look or even if they have a hot meal. The addict's domicile becomes a vacant building, an abandon vehicle, or some alleyway that is infested with rats. If they're lucky they may find shelter for the night with a trick they just met.

There is only one thing that the addict needs or wants, and that is their next fix of heroin or cocaine. How they get the money really does not matter. If there are no funds to support one's habit then crime is often the alternative. In this section of the book you will see just how Maryland rates among other states on crime; and a lot of the crime is due to drug addiction.

As a police officer I arrested an addict for beating an elderly lady over the head with a trashcan lid just so he could take her pocketbook. His intention was not to hurt the lady; it was only to get money for his seemingly endless craving for heroin. Sadly, this violent act caused the elderly lady to die from head injuries and the young user was arrested for homicide.

Another arrest I made was this young girl, she told me that her addiction to heroin made her a streetwalker; better know as a prostitute. She said her heroin addiction was feeding another person's sex addiction. I never thought about it like that before, but she was right. Our society seems to feed off one another, especially when people are trapped in a situation like addiction. This same girl told me how she had been treated with so much disrespect; that after the sexual fling she felt like taking her own life.

Richard was the father of a beautiful son; young Richard was only seven years old when a man who was fleeing from police because of a simple traffic violation hit him and snuffed out his life. Who would have guessed that the fleeing drivers was so high on PCP that he never even noticed the horrible act that he had committed.

I recall the story of the man who police arrested for disorderly conduct and was placed in central lock-up. He was only there for a few moments when the turnkey just happened to notice blood coming from his cell. This guy was so high on LSD that he poked out both of his eyes using his index fingers.

A drug deal went bad off Blair Road late one summer night. So in retaliation a bomb was place under a car. When the driver got into the car and started it up the entire vehicle blew up. The man in the car somehow lived but for the rest of his life he would live without both of his legs.

It is a know fact in Baltimore that you can get an addict to do almost anything for a few dollars; even if it means busting someone's head open, setting a fire, breaking a window, or even beating a person up. They really don't care about anyone's life. They only care about the next fix.

In the late stages of drug use you can bet the user has already experienced fear, and for him or her to commit a crime for someone else for a few dollars is no big deal.

How Maryland Ranks With Other Cities In The U.S.A.

In the year 2000 God saw fit to place 5,296,486 people in Maryland, which ranked the state 19th in population. * The following information came from the Disaster Center's Website for Maryland.

For violent crime Maryland had a report incident rate of 786.6 per 100,000 people, this ranked Maryland 3rd highest among the states.

For crimes against property the state had reported incident rate of 4,029.5 per 100,000 people, this ranked the state 17th highest with other states.

Murder in Maryland had a report incident rate of 8.1 murders per 100,000 people, this rank Maryland 3rd highest with other states.

Maryland's 29.1 reported forced rapes per 100,000 people, ranked Maryland 30th on the list with other states.

Robbery in Maryland per 100,000 people was 256.0, which ranked Maryland number 1 in robberies with other states.

Aggravated assaults per 100,000 people was 493.3, which rated Maryland 5th for this crime with other states.

Burglaries for every 100,000 people was 744.4, which ranked Maryland 21st on the list with other states.

Larceny reported 2,745.2 times per 100,000 people ranked Maryland 19th with other states.

Vehicle theft occurred 539.5 times per 100,000 people, which ranked Maryland 6th with other states.

- According to a report "Talk Left.com" Infectious diseases are raising in our prisons.
- Nearly one in three inmates entering into the system is infected with HIV, syphilis, hepatitis B virus, or hepatitis C virus; many of them with one or more infections according to blood survey by state health officials.

The Court System

I will never forget being in a courtroom in Baltimore City and waiting for the judge to come out. The courtroom was filled and people were standing in the isle along the wall because both witnesses and criminals already occupied the seats.

After waiting for twenty minutes for the judge to come out, he opens the door and the bailiff says "all rise". The judge sets down and has this obnoxious look on his face. He then starts insulting everyone in the courtroom by saying, "you people did not stand up fast enough for me, so we will do this again". He then gets up and walks out of the courtroom. THEN, the bailiff says to the people in the courtroom again, "all rise". The judge walks back like he was in the Miss America Pageant but he is still not satisfied and told the people that they had to do it a third time; so on the third try and thirty minutes later court started.

Then we play the postponement game; anyone who wanted a postponement could get one; it could be for any reason. After that game we played the "I don't have an attorney game"; anyone who needed an attorney would get a postponement to get an attorney. Then we played the "I want a jury trial game"; if someone did not like the setting judge they could get a jury trial. Then we had to break for the judge; that was another twenty minutes. After two hours of games, court starts and then came the biggest waste of time of the day. The defendants all got slaps on the hands for the crimes they committed and were then sent to an already over worked probation department. There was no real jail time for the crimes they committed. EVERYTHING was probation. What message does that send to offenders? Look at the record for each state and judge for yourself.

This is a report from * *Capital News Service, Wednesday, April 23, 2003*

Washington – Most counties saw some of the drug sentences handed down by their circuit court judge's fall below recommended sentencing guidelines from 1999 – 2001. But a disproportionate number of drug cases in Baltimore, and a push by courts there for alternative sentences, help drive the state average of below – guideline sentences to 57 percent according to state sentencing statistics. The numbers do not include district court cases or municipal – charge cases.

County	Drug sentences	Below Guidelines	Percent Below Guidelines
Allegany	59	19	32.2
Anne Arundel	632	258	40.8
Balt. City	8,532	6,438	75.5
Baltimore	915	333	36.4
Calvert	69	23	33.3
Caroline	50	10	20.0
Carroll	56	20	35.7
Cecil	114	28	24.6
Charles	155	28	24.6
Dorchester	146	11	7.5
Fredrick	362	166	45.8
Garrett	0	0	0
Harford	115	29	25.2
Howard	134	44	32.8
Kent	62	16	25.8
Montgomery	344	151	43.9
Prince George's	1,119	329	29.4
Queen Anne's	27	2	7.4
St, Mary's	92	21	22.8
Somerset	79	10	12.7
Talbot	104	14	13.5
Washington	534	85	15.9
Wicomico	327	34	10.4
Worcester	151	24	15.9

My research shows that some laws are not even enforced, and are you ready for this? Some people are not even aware that this law exists when in fact they are being paid to know the law.

I am going to write this just as I have found in it the News Briefs titled *"Politician-Touted Maryland Drug Law is Not Used"*. In 1990, then Maryland Governor William Donald Schaefer (D) signed an anti-drug bill called the first of its kind in the country. The law gave state agencies the power to revoke the license of any professional convicted of a drug offense (Charles Babington, "High-Profile Drug Bill Became Low Impact Md. Law," Washington Past, June 9, 1997, p A1). [This is the typical hyperbole, exaggeration or dishonesty endemic to anti-drug proposals. In the Anti-Drug Abuse Act of 1988 (P.L. 100-690 Congress required that all federal licenses be stripped from persons convicted of drug offenses (Sec. 5301). – EES]

Seven years later, a survey by the Washington Post reveals that the law has not been used. The survey asked officials at all major Maryland agencies about the impact of the law Schaefer once called part of the "best drug bills of any state in the union." Several officials said they did not know of the law at all, and no one could confirm that it had ever been put to use in revoking a license. The law took effect January 1, 1991, and since then NO ONE has lost their license because of the law.

Drug convictions in Maryland have ranged from 11,906 to 13,245 annually during the years the law has been in effect. BUT Maryland Delegate D. Bruce Pool (D-Washington County, who helped draft the bill, attributes the bill's failure to society's attitude toward drug-users. "I can't say I'm astounded," he said. "The bill was passed in the heyday of zero tolerance, and since then, we've seen a swing against some of the harsher results of the policy."

What does this law mean? The law gives the right to state agencies to revoke the licenses of any professional. IF CONVICTED of a drug offense. The word "right" means they can revoke. And the word "IF" in this state means they most likely will get probation before judgment. Simply meaning the chances for a conviction are not good.

So let's take a situation that most of us has been effected by in one-way or the other. Pain pills and the doctors who hand them out knowing full well they are being abused.

I know of countless people who have been hooked on pain pills; some of them have died others are living in a hellish nightmare. Families are going through hell because of this. And our society applauds these doctors who give prescriptions out to patients when it's not necessary and for WHAT? It's all for the money, the greed, and the attitude that they will never get caught. But YOU can help stop this abuse today and here is how you do it.

- Call the doctor's office and ask to speak the doctor. If the secretary does not put him or her on the phone then give them a message. Tell them who you are and what is going on with your family member or friend and that you want the abuse stopped today.
- Make it clear that if it does not stop TODAY you will call the police and every agency in the state to let them know about this activity.
- In addition, let all parties know you will also hold them responsible if any thing happens to your love one.
- Let everyone know when YOU plan to call the police and make a report. This could win the battle for you right there.
- If you make a police report ask the officers for the CC# (complaint number). You will want a copy of the report for your investigation when you call state agencies.
- Remember, your just putting the fear of God into the parties involved so that the abuse will stop.
- Always get names of the people you talk to. Keep a notebook of dates and times of calls or visits.
- Keep calling, send letters, and have some other family member do the same. You just may be surprised at the results.
- Remember, if you go to the office be polite and carry a recorder with you. Let everyone know your taping the conversation.

- If you are told not to call the office again STOP calling.
- If go to the office in person take a friend with you. Ask to see the doctor and start talking about the abuse in front of others; I am sure the doctor will see you. IF the police are called remember you MUST be polite and orderly. Do you think the doctor will call the police for an orderly person? And would he do it in front of his other patients? I don't think so. If he does, the police will ask you to leave or be arrested. I suggest you leave. You now have made your point.

Most doctors are very efficient and professional; if you let them know of your concerns in a nice way, I think you will get results.

When I found out that my son was seeing a doctor and getting pain pills from him I called the doctor. I made it very clear that I was upset about what was going on and that if it did not stop coming after him; I also advised them I was retired narcotics officer. The doctor's reply was, "OK I can't see him any longer". That piece of dross is no longer my son's suppler. And it only took one call.

Here is a game played by most attorneys. If a witness comes to court for the first time it is probable that a postponement will be requested. YOU must remember how the games are played. They try and wear witnesses down, so be prepared for a postponement before you get to court. Here are some things to remember when you testify in a case.

- Always be on time.
- Dress like a professional.
- When you're asked a question, keep the answer short and to the point. However, if the opposing attorney asks a question try and answer it with a simple yes or no. Do not give any additional information.
- If you don't know, say I don't know. Don't give excuses.
- If something is not clear in a question, ask the attorney or judge to repeat the question.
- Use the words "Yes Sir, No Sir." Always show respect to all parties involved.

- If you must refer to a notebook, and you are asked why you kept one simple say, "I wanted to remember the event so I put it in my notebook. (like a police report) You are with in your rights.
- Look the attorneys in the eyes and answer the questions with certainty.
- Remember the job of the opposing attorney is to make you look bad. However, if you follow these guidelines things will go very well for you.
- When you finish your testimony leave them with these words "Thank You".
- Remember to always wait for about five-ten seconds before you answer a question. This gives your attorney time to object if he needs to, and it gives you time to think of your answer after the question is asked.
- Never answer a question in a tone of anger; and remember to smile and look friendly.

The following information will help you to understand the courts system. I have many students that want to know about court proceedings. And what certain courts can or cannot do.

- Traffic court is self-explanatory, however, if you have a criminal charge along with a traffic charge the judge can hear both the traffic and the criminal at the same time, as long as the criminal charge is not a felony. Traffic court is held in the same room as criminal court but on a certain day of the week.
- District court, a judge in the district court cannot hear a criminal felony case. These cases are sent to Circuit Court and usually follow an arraignment. An arraignment is a simple hearing to see if you have an attorney and understand the charges that have been place on you. This is NOT a trial.
- Your right to an attorney, a smart man never defends himself. You have the right to an attorney ever time you face a judge. If you cannot afford an attorney the state will appoint one to you. YOU MUST go to legal aid right after

you have been charged so the paper work can be in order and a lawyer assigned to you. DO NOT take any charge lightly. And Yes, all attorneys from legal aid have passed the bar exam and are qualified to handle your case. The judge likes to see people have taken the responsibility to obtain counsel before they come into the courtroom. Here are the phone numbers in Maryland 410-951-7777 this is the main number. The hotline number is 410-951-7750 for seniors 410-951-7760. This service has been in effect in Maryland since 1911 and is statewide.

- You can appeal district court cases and they will be moved to the circuit courts. However, appeals from the circuit courts become more difficult.

According to the DEA newsletter for Maryland, the population is 5,296,486, there are 14,767 law enforcement officers, the state prison population is 22,969 and the probation population is around 81,286.

Maryland is rated number two (2) in violent crime nationally. With these stats we can see why we spend the day in court and the sad part about it is that most of our crime emerges from the state's drug problem.

How Bad Is Maryland's Drug Problem

This is a report from the *National Drug Intelligence Center, Maryland Drug Treatment Assessment August 2002, Document ID # 2002 – SO379MD - 001

Heroin: poses the most serious drug threat to Maryland. Rates of abuse are high, particularly in Baltimore. Heroin is readily available in urban parts of the state and is becoming increasingly available in suburban and rural areas.

While heroin abuse typically is not associated with violent crime, violence related to the distribution of heroin is a serious problem in Baltimore.

Maryland-based local independent dealers and Dominican and Colombian criminal groups based in New York City and Philadelphia are the dominant transporters of heroin into Maryland.

Local independent dealers and loosely organized gangs dominate retail heroin distribution throughout the state. In Baltimore, loosely organized neighborhood gangs consisting primarily of African American members conduct most of the retail heroin distribution.

Heroin Abuse: Maryland, particularly Baltimore, has one of the most serious heroin abuse problems in the nation. Rates of heroin abuse continue to increase throughout the state, and rates of abuse in Baltimore have reached very high levels. According to Maryland Drug Early Warning System Drug Scan, a statewide, county-level project designed to obtain perceptions of local drug trends from substance abuse professionals, heroin is a primary drug of abuse in Baltimore where there is an estimated 45,000 heroin addicts.

City health officials attribute increases in heroin-related admissions in Baltimore to the increased availability of treatment facilities. Statewide funding for treatment facilities increased from $18 million in 1997 to $46 million in 2000.

According to mortality data from DAWN, in the Baltimore metropolitan area, the number of deaths in which heroin/morphine was a factor increased from 302 in 1996 to 451 in 1999, then decreased to 397 in 2000.

The availability of high purity heroin at retail level is at least partly responsible for the number of fatal heroin overdoses in Maryland. Inexperienced new abusers who have not developed a tolerance often overdose because of the high purity. Even experienced abusers may misjudge their dosage and overdose because of the higher purity of heroin.

According to the Drug Enforcement Administration (DEA), the high purity heroin affects newly released prison inmates who were heroin abusers before their incarceration. They often revert to their old habits, not realizing that the heroin they purchase is now much more potent than before.

In 1999 for the first time, more residents of Baltimore died as a result of drug overdose than as a result of homicide, part of a disturbing trend in which overdose deaths in Maryland nearly tripled in a decade. * *Source, The Baltimore Sun, 16 September 2000.*

Heroin abuse among young people in Maryland decreased slightly from 1998 through 2001. The 2001 Maryland Adolescent Survey, modeled after the Monitoring the Future study, reports a slight decline from 1998 through 2001 in the percentage of sixth, eighth, tenth, and twelfth grade students who reported having abused heroin in the past 30 days. This decline followed an increase from 1996 through 1998 for sixth, eighth, and tenth grade students. Heroin abuse among twelfth grade students declined steadily from 1996 through 2001.

Heroin abuse is prevalent throughout most areas in Maryland. Heroin was a primary drug of abuse, an emerging drug of abuse, or a drug of concern in 18 of the 23 counties and Baltimore in 2000, according to the Maryland Drug Early Warning System Drug Scan.

Availability: Heroin is readily available in urban areas in Maryland, especially in Baltimore, and is increasingly available throughout suburban and rural parts of the state. In response to the National Drug Intelligence Center (NDIC) National Drug Threat Survey 2001, the Maryland State Police reported that the availability of heroin is increasing in Maryland and is spreading from the cities to suburban areas.

South American heroin is the type most commonly available in Maryland; however, Southeast Asian and Southwest Asian heroin occasionally are available. The availability of Mexican heroin is limited.

According to DEA from the first quarter of 2002, through the first quarter of 2002 there was little change in heroin prices in the Baltimore area. During that time, heroin sold for $10.00 to $20.00 per bag. The average price of a gram decreased slightly from $105 to $102, while the price of an ounce remained $2,800. Wholesale prices decreased slightly from $92,500 per kilogram in the first quarter of 2002, to $90,000 in the first quarter of 2002.

The number of heroin-related investigations has increased in Maryland. Maryland state and local law enforcement respondents to the National Drug Threat Survey 2001 reported that the number of heroin-related investigations increased over the previous year (1999). From October 1998 through June of 2001, 50 of the 173 Organized Crime Drug Enforcement Task Force investigations often involve more than one drug type.

The amount of heroin seized by federal law enforcement agencies remained relatively stable from 1998 to 2000; however, the number of highway seizures decreased from 1999 to 2000. According to Federal-Wide Drug Seizure (FDSS) data, federal law enforcement agencies in Maryland seized 10 kilograms of heroin in 1998, 9.7 kilograms in 1999, and 10.1 kilograms in 2000.

Violence: Heroin distributors at all levels in Baltimore commit violent crimes to protect their turf and to expand their drug distribution operation. Dominican criminal groups in the region commit violent crimes to assert and maintain dominance over drug distribution territories and to control retail distributors Heroin abusers frequently commit property crimes - including random theft, credit fraud, and burglary - to support their addictions.

Production: Opium is not produced nor is it cultivated in Maryland. Heroin is produced primarily in four regions, South America, Mexico, Southeast Asia, and Southwest Asia. Most of the heroin available in Maryland is produced in South America. Although, limited amounts from Southeast and Southwest Asia are available. The Baltimore County Narcotics Unit reports that some heroin dealers are milling heroin in the county and transporting it to the city of Baltimore for distribution.

Heroin Milling: Bulk heroin usually is milled before being distributed at the retail level. Milling is a process by which bulk heroin is cut with diluents such as *lactose and *mannitol or adulterants such as caffeine and then divided into individual doses that often are packaged in glassine bags. Often, multiple glassine bags are packages together for retail sale. One kilogram of nearly 100% pure heroin can be cut and divided into approximately 30,000 glassine bags.

- Mannitol, a white crystalline, water-soluble, slightly sweet alcohol $C6 - H8 - (Ho6)$ used as a dietary supplement and dietetic sweetener and in medical tests for renal function.
- Lactose, a disaccharide $C12 - H22-O11$ found in milk; that may be hydrolyzed to yield glucose and galactose. A white crystalline substance obtained from whey and used in infant foods, bakery products, confections, and pharmaceuticals as a diluent and excipient. Also called milk sugar.

Transportation: Maryland – based local independent dealers and Dominican and Colombian criminal groups based in New York City and Philadelphia are the dominant transporters of heroin into Maryland. These independent dealers and criminal groups primarily travel via private or rental vehicles on interstate highways or via public transportation (buses and trains). Heroin is also transported into Maryland via commercial aircraft and maritime vessels.

Criminal groups generally employ couriers to transport heroin into the state. Local independent dealers who distribute wholesale quantities in Maryland typically travel to primary distribution centers such as New York and Philadelphia to purchase heroin from Dominican criminal groups. They then transport the drug back to Maryland. Miami is also a distribution center for wholesale quantities of heroin available in Maryland. Heroin abusers and independent retail distributors throughout Maryland travel to Baltimore, Salisbury, Philadelphia, and Washington, D.C. to purchase small quantities of heroin for personal use and local retail distribution.

Couriers primarily transport heroin into and through the state in automobiles and buses traveling on I-95. These couriers sometimes use alternate, less traveled routes to avoid highway interdiction. These couriers travel US-13 to US-50 and then I-97 to Baltimore, or follow US-13 to areas along Eastern Shore. According to EPIC Pipeline and Convoy data. Interstates 97, 495, and 695; US-140 and US-24 are also used to transport heroin into and within the state.

Heroin is also smuggled directly into Maryland by couriers on commercial airline flights. West African criminal groups, primarily Nigerian, employ couriers to transport heroin into Baltimore / Washington International Airport. The couriers take advantage of international flights such as twice-weekly commercial flights from Ghana. The couriers transport heroin either in or on their bodies or in their luggage (which allows for the transportation of larger quantities). On August 20, 2000, U.S. Customs Service inspectors at Baltimore / Washington International Airport arrested a Nigerian national who had ingested 82 pellets containing a total of 1 kilogram of heroin. On August 27, 2000 a British national who had ingested 78 pellets containing 936 grams of heroin was also arrested at Baltimore / Washington International Airport. He had arrived on a Ghana Airways flight from Nigeria.

Heroin has been smuggled into Maryland through the Port of Baltimore but to a much lesser extent than by land or air. The DEA Washington Division reports that small quantities of Southwest Asian heroin are transported to Baltimore area through the Port of Baltimore. In 1998, the USCS seized multi-gram quantities of Southwest Asian heroin from crewmembers aboard Pakistani ships entering the Port of Baltimore. The heroin in these shipments usually was destined for distribution in Pakistani communities in Prince George's and western Anne Arundel Counties.

Distribution: Dominican and Colombian criminal groups based in New York City, Philadelphia, and Baltimore and Maryland-based local independent dealers dominate the wholesale distribution of heroin in Maryland. Some Dominican criminals have established part-time residency in the Maryland cities where they distribute heroin. Wholesale heroin distribution in Maryland is centered in Baltimore. Local independent dealers may distribute heroin at the wholesale level in the counties around the city of Baltimore; however, the Maryland State Police indicate there are no known wholesale disturbers outside the Baltimore area.

Baltimore serves as the primary distribution city for heroin in Maryland. Salisbury, located along major smuggling route US-13, serves as a secondary distribution city for Eastern Maryland.

Law enforcement officials have identified a link between Latin Kings gang members from New York City and retail distributors of heroin in Salisbury. Salisbury officials have seized bags of heroin bearing stamps that resemble those sold by Latin Kings in New York City.

Local independent dealers and loosely organized, largely African American gangs, are the dominant retail distributors of heroin in Maryland. According to Baltimore City Narcotics Unit, many retail distributors purchase heroin in wholesale quantities, transport it to private residences in Baltimore County suburbs, cut and package it into retail quantities, and transport the heroin to Baltimore city for retail distribution. Many abusers also distribute heroin at the retail level, and those living in suburban and rural areas of Maryland often travel to Baltimore, Salisbury, and Philadelphia, to purchase 12 to 13 bags of heroin for approximately $100. They use 2 to 3 bags themselves, and distribute the remainder to their friends for as much as $20 a bag.

Cocaine: The distribution and abuse of cocaine- both powder and crack-pose a significant threat to Maryland. Cocaine is frequently abused and readily available in the state, particularly in the Baltimore area. Crake cocaine is the drug most commonly associated with violent crime in Maryland. Dominican and Colombian criminal groups based in New York City, Philadelphia, and Maryland-based local independent dealers are the primary transporters of powdered cocaine into Maryland. These Dominican, and to a lesser extent Colombian criminal groups supply wholesale and retail distributors throughout the state. Jamaican criminal groups, African American gangs, and local independent dealers distribute cocaine at wholesale and midlevel. At a retail level, loosely organized African Americans gangs and local independent dealers distribute powdered and crack cocaine.

Abuse: The abuse of cocaine is a significant threat to Maryland. According to data from the NHSDA, in 1999 the percentage of Maryland residents who reported using cocaine in the year prior to the survey (1.6%) was comparable to the national percentage (1.7%).

Cocaine-related admissions to publicly funded facilities in Maryland remain high despite a steady decrease since 1994. According to TEDS data, cocaine-related treatment admissions decreased from 10,433 in 1994 to 7,571 in 1999. This is the number of admissions per 100,000 population in Maryland, the fifth highest in the nation in 1999.

Each year from 1994 through 1999, there were more admissions for cocaine abuse than for any other illicit drug except heroin.

In Baltimore, according to mortality data from DAWN, the numbers of cocaine-related deaths where cocaine was a factor increased from 266 in 1996, to 311 in 1998 then decreased to 243 in 2000. In 2000 most of the deaths (178) occurred in the city of Baltimore.

The percentage of Maryland residents aged 18 and under reporting cocaine abuse has decreased in recent years. In 2001 Maryland Adolescent Survey reported that the percentage of sixth, eighth, and tenth grade students reporting that they had abused the powder or crack cocaine in the 30 days prior to the survey increased from 1996 through 1998, then decreased from 1998 through 2001.

Availability: Powdered cocaine and crack cocaine are readily available throughout Maryland. Respondents to the NDIC National Drug Threat Survey 2001 reported that the availability of cocaine is moderate to high. Of the 20 respondents, 8 reported that the availability of powdered cocaine was high and 9 reported that the availability was moderate; 15 reported that the availability of crack cocaine was high and 4 reported the availability was moderate.

Prices for powered and crack cocaine are relativity stable in Maryland, and purity levels vary widely. Maryland State Police reported that powered cocaine sold throughout the state for $50 to $120 per gram and $18,000 to $25,000 per kilogram in the first half of 2000. They also reported that crack cocaine sold for $10 to $50 per rock, $80 to $100 per gram, and $800 to $1000 per ounce. In 2001, DEA reported that in the Baltimore area powered cocaine sold for $80 to $100 per gram and crack sold for $100 per gram. The Maryland State Police reported that statewide the purity of powered cocaine ranged from 37 percent to 95 percent in 2000. Data on the purity of crack cocaine were unavailable.

The high number of cocaine – related investigations at the federal, state, and local levels reflects the ready availability. Twelve of twenty Maryland State and local law enforcement respondents to the NDIC National Drug Threat Survey 2001 reported conducting 340 powdered cocaine and 2,267 crack cocaine investigations in 1999.

The amount of powered and crack cocaine seized in Maryland has fluctuated since 1998. According to FDSS data, federal law enforcement agencies in Maryland seized 129.0 kilograms of cocaine in 1998, 96.7 kilograms in 1999, and 132.1 kilograms in 2000.

Six of eighteen respondents to NDIC National Drug Threat Survey 2001 reported seizing more powered cocaine in 2000 than in 1999, while 5 reported the amount of powered cocaine seized remained the same. Eight of 17 law enforcement agencies reported an increase in the amount of crack cocaine seized, while 7 reported that the amount seized remained the same.

The percentage of federal sentences related to cocaine violations in Maryland was higher than the national percentage in 2000. The number of cocaine-related sentences was higher than any other drug. According to the USSC, approximately 73% of drug related federal sentences in Maryland 2000 were cocaine – related, compared with 44% nationwide.

Violence: Crack cocaine is the drug most associated with violent crime in Maryland. Abusers often commit violent crimes in order to support their habits and distributors sometimes use violence to protect their turf. The Baltimore area, in particular, has experienced significant violence associated with cocaine distribution. In June of 2001, three men were convicted of the 1999 murder of five women in Baltimore during a dispute over crack cocaine. One of the women allegedly sold another substance to men in place of cocaine.

Production: Cocaine is not cultivated nor is cocaine produced in Maryland. However, many African American independent dealers transport powdered cocaine into Maryland and convert cocaine locally at residence in urban areas. Local conversion is largely in response to federal sentencing guidelines, which mandate more stringent penalties for possessing crack than powered cocaine.

Federal Cocaine Distribution Penalties: Under current federal law, a person convicted of distributing 5 grams of crack cocaine faces a mandatory sentence of 5 years in prison; this is equivalent to the penalty for distributing 500 grams of powered cocaine.

Transportation: Dominican and to the lesser extent, Colombian criminal groups based in New York City and Philadelphia, and Maryland – based local independent dealers, primarily African Americans, are the dominate transporters of powered cocaine into and through Maryland. These groups and independent dealers transport most of the cocaine into Maryland using automobiles, buses, and rail systems. Cocaine arrives at

Baltimore / Washington International Airport and the Port of Baltimore often is destined for locations outside the state, although some remains in Maryland.

Criminal groups often employ couriers to transport cocaine into Maryland in automobiles and buses on I95. Some reports indicate that couriers also use alternate, less traveled routes to avoid highway interdiction. Transporters use US-13 US-50 I-97 Interstate 70 and 81 and US-301 to transport cocaine into and through the state.

Jet Way Task Force Officers Seize Cocaine: On January 5, 2000, Baltimore Operation Jet Way Task Force officers seized 300 grams of cocaine and arrested a male resident of New York City. He was traveling by bus on a one-way ticket from New York City to Baltimore. The cocaine was found concealed inside the suspects carry – on backpack. The suspect told law enforcement officers that he had been paid $350 to take the cocaine to Baltimore and deliver it to an unknown male.

Cocaine is also transported into the state on international flights through Baltimore / Washington International Airport. In May of 2001 Baltimore Operation Jet Way Task Force officers seized 2.4 kilograms of cocaine and 3.8 kilograms of marijuana from separate packages that were shipped from Mesa, Arizona, Inglewood, California, and Boulder, Colorado. A controlled delivery was conducted on the package from Mesa resulting in the arrest of a male suspect in Washington D.C. Cocaine is the drug most often seized by law enforcement officers at the Port of Baltimore. Over 95 kilograms of cocaine were seized in two separate incidents in 1998. One involved a seizure of 56 kilograms and another a seizure of 39 kilograms from Philippine nationals. In November of 1998, 450 kilograms of cocaine were seized in Lebanon, Pennsylvania. The cocaine, packed in green plastic bundles and concealed inside a large bolt-cutting machine, had been transported through the Port of Baltimore from Caracas, Venezuela.

Distribution: Dominican, and to a lesser extent, Colombian criminal groups based in New York City and Philadelphia supply wholesale and retail distributors throughout the State of Maryland. At the wholesale level, Jamaican criminal groups, African American gangs, and local independent dealers distribute cocaine.

Local independent dealers as well as loosely organized African American gangs convert some powered cocaine to crack cocaine locally and are the dominant retail powered and crack cocaine distributors in Maryland. Local dealers from all economic backgrounds and suburban rural areas often travel to urban areas to purchase cocaine for distribution in their areas.

Marijuana: Marijuana is the most readily available, commonly abused, illicit drug in Maryland. Most of the marijuana available in the state is produced in Mexico; however, marijuana produced in Maryland is available to a lesser extent. Local independent dealers, primarily Caucasians, cultivate cannabis indoors and outdoors. Mexican criminal groups transport lesser amounts into the state. Jamaican criminal groups are the dominant wholesale distributors of marijuana produced in Mexico.

Abuse: Marijuana is the most widely abused illegal drug in Maryland, the rate of marijuana abuse in the state is comparable to the national average. According to the 1999 NHSDA, 4.9 percent of individuals surveyed in Maryland reported having abused marijuana in the previous month compared with 4.7 percent nationwide. Most individuals reporting past month marijuana abuse were between the ages of 18 and 25.

Maryland marijuana-related admissions to publicly funded treatment facilities increased from 4,644 in 1994 to 7,196 in 1996 then steadily decreased to 6,862 in 1999. According to TEDS, The Maryland Alcohol and Drug Abuse Administration, approximately 64 percent of marijuana abusers admitted for treatment in 1997 first abused the drug between the ages of 12 and 17. The Maryland Alcohol and Drug Abuse Administration reported that in 1998, drug abuse screenings detected marijuana abuse in 86.4 percent of admissions for individuals aged 17 and younger at Maryland substances abuse treatment programs. Many used marijuana in conjunction with other drugs.

Teenagers in Maryland abuse marijuana more frequently than any other illicit drug. A November 2000 report by the Drug Early Warning Systems indicates that marijuana was the primary drug detected among juveniles arrested in Maryland. According to the 2001 Maryland Adolescent Survey, 37.9 percent of twelfth grade students reported having abused marijuana in the past year, more than triple the percent that reported having used ecstasy, which was the next highest abused at 10.9 percent. The survey further indicates that the percentage of sixth, eighth, tenth, and twelfth grade students who reported marijuana abuse in the past 30 days was lower in 2001 than in 1998.

Availability: Marijuana is widely available throughout the state. Prices for the drug vary because marijuana with higher levels of THC (tetrahydrocannabinnl) typically commands a higher price. In Maryland, Mexico – produced commercial – marijuana, which is made from the whole cannabis plant and has an average THC content of 5.5 percent, sold for $160 to $200 per ounce and $1,000 to $1,200 per pound in 2000, according to the Maryland State Police. Sinsemilla, which typically is produced using only the leaves and buds of the un-pollinated female plant, sold for $200 to $600 per ounce and $1,500 to $3,000 per pound.

Investigation by state and local law enforcement agencies and seizures by state and federal law enforcement agencies reflect the wide availability of marijuana in the Maryland. The National Drug Threat Survey 2001 reported having conducted 470 marijuana – related investigations in 1999. The Maryland State Police reported an increase in statewide cannabis seizers from 3,474 plants in 1998 to 3,610 plants in 1999 to 6,954 plants in 2000.

Violence: A significant amount of violent crime associated with marijuana distribution has occurred in Baltimore. Baltimore City Police report that violence related to marijuana distribution is increasing. Baltimore County Police officials report that in December 2001 a dispute over marijuana led to the fatal shooting of a teenager at Owings Mills Mall.

Production: Most marijuana that is available in Maryland is produced in Mexico. However, indoor cultivation is increasing because the quality of the marijuana obtained from indoor grows tends to be higher and the drug commands a higher price. Outdoor cultivation is common during the summer months, especially on the Eastern Shore. In Caroline County on the Eastern Shore, the Sheriff's Officer reported in 2000 that most of the marijuana sold in its jurisdiction was locally grown, primarily outdoors.

Transportation: Mexican produced marijuana is transshipped through California and southwestern states. Jamaican criminal groups are the dominant transporters of marijuana into Maryland; Mexican criminal groups transport lesser amounts into the state. Jamaican criminal groups usually purchase marijuana from Mexican criminal groups in the southwestern United States and transport it primarily via package delivery services into Maryland. Although transportation by automobile, bus, and airlines does occur. According to the Prince George's County Police Department, California is the primary source of marijuana available in its jurisdiction, and packaged delivery services is the primary method used to transport marijuana into the county. According to DEA, criminal elements among Mexican migrant farmers working on Maryland's Eastern Shore transport marijuana into that area, usually by automobile.

Marijuana usually is transported into Maryland in 5 – 14 pound packages. On February 22, 2000, Operation Jet Way Task Force officers at Baltimore / Washington International Airport seized a package containing 10.6 pounds of marijuana sent from El Cajon, California. The marijuana was shrink-wrapped, concealed with dryer sheets, and placed in a plastic storage container.

Distribution: Jamaican criminal groups are the dominant wholesale distributors of marijuana in Maryland. The Montgomery County Police Department indicate in 2000 that Jamaican criminal groups are the principal distributors of marijuana to high school students in that county. The Pagan's Motorcycle Club, with chapters in Anne Arundel County and the cities of Baltimore, Ocean City, and Frederick, is predominant in the state and frequently distributes marijuana. Street gangs also distribute marijuana in addition to other drugs. In Maryland, marijuana often is sold in "blunt", hollowed – out cigars that are filled with marijuana or combination of marijuana and tobacco. In Baltimore, law enforcement authorities occasionally seize marijuana sprinkled with PCP (phencyclidine). Other drugs of abuse will be discussed in depth later on in this book.

If you would like information about your state's drug problem you may call or write the following agencies.

National Drug Intelligence Center
319 Washing Street, 5th Floor
Johnstown, PA 15901
814-532-4601
Fax 814-532-4690

National Drug Intelligence Center
8201 Greensboro Drive, Suite 1001
McLean, VA 22101 – 3840
703-556-8970
Fax 703-556-7807

You Be The Judge

With nearly 5.3 million residents, Maryland is the nineteenth most populous state. With approximately 542 persons per square mile, it is the sixth most densely populated state. The average income for middle class as of 2000 is $51,685. The unemployment rate as of 2000 is 3.9%. The land area is 9,775 square miles and the shoreline is 3,190 miles. In addition to all of this beauty we also have the not so charming facts of drug addiction. Here are the facts supporting my statement. The following are Drug – Related Treatment Admissions to Public Funded Facilities from Maryland 1994 – 1999. The source U.S. Department of Health and Human Services, Substances Abuse and Mental Health Services Administration, Treatment Episode Data Sheet. The total includes all drug and alcohol related treatment admissions.

Heroin:
1994 – 11,741 addicts found public funding for treatment
1995 – 13,457 addicts found public funding for treatment
1996 – 13,049 addicts found public funding for treatment
1997 – 14,077 addicts found public funding for treatment
1998 – 15,032 addicts found public funding for treatment
1999 – 15,823 addicts found public funding for treatment

Cocaine:
1994 – 10,433 addicts found public funding for treatment
1995 – 10,007 addicts found public funding for treatment
1996 – 9,325 addicts found public funding for treatment
1997 – 8,142 addicts found public funding for treatment
1999 – 7,571 addicts found public funding for treatment

Marijuana:

1994 – 4,644 addicts found public funding for treatment
1995 – 6,533 addicts found public funding for treatment
1996 – 7,196 addicts found public funding for treatment
1997 – 7,090 addicts found public funding for treatment
1998 – 8,142 addicts found public funding for treatment
1999 – 6,862 addicts found public funding for treatment

Total number that went into public funding facilities:

1994 – 56,885	1996 – 57,681	1998 – 57,358
1995 – 59,091	1997 – 58,058	1999 – 56,161

Does Maryland have a drug problem? It is my opinion that we do; and that we have lost the war on drugs. Now some may disagree because of their research and numbers that you find in their reports. But if you think the number of addiction is going down because of the above report YOU are mistaken.

Many people are being turned away from treatment programs; the waiting list is too long or the person addicted gets the runaround on the telephone. The political dross slinging about how we are doing so much for people who are addicted is the biggest monkeyshine story of 2004.

I now teach a drug / alcohol education program; I have tried to find help for some of my students that needed treatment, and like always my request falls to deaf ears. Forty-four of my students have passed away and I will always believe if some would have been in treatment they would be here today.

Ask anyone who is addicted and has no insurance just how hard it is to find an inpatient program; and they will tell you it is nearly impossible. What we have in our society is summed up in one word, GREED. If you do not have money for treatment then you're out of luck. If you have insurance then you are treated for thirty days or less; or to put it simply until the insurance runs out.

You can make a difference; call your state officials and ask them to help Maryland provide a treatment program for people who really want to find help and have no insurance.

Chapter Two
The Facts About Drugs And Drug Abuse

Facts About Drugs

Fact: Drug and drug – using behaviors are linked to crime in several ways according to the National Drug Control Policy (ONDCP). The following information comes from the White House Office of National Drug Control Policy.

- It is a crime to use, possess, manufacture, or distribute drugs classified as illegal.
- The effects of drug-related behavior-violence as effect of drug use, robberies to get money to buy drugs, violence against rival traffickers- influence society daily.
- In 1999, approximately 6.3 million adults – 3.1% of the Nations adult population-were under correctional supervision. (That is, incarceration, probation, or parole). Additionally, 98,913 juveniles (9% of whom were drug offenders) were incarceration in public or private juvenile facilities for non-status offenders. Drug offender's account for 21% (236,800) of the state prison population in 1998, up from 6% in 1980.
- The F.B.I. reported 580,900 arrests for drug offenders in 1980. The number of arrest peaked at 1,559,100 in 1997. In 1999 there were 1,532,200-drug arrest.
- The Bureau of Justice Statistics (BJS) and the n=National Center on Addiction and Substance Abuse (CASA) estimate that from 60% to 80% of the Nation's correctional population have used drugs at some point in their lives.
- In 1997, 82,646 and 993,365 male inmates were in Federal and State prisons, respectively, and 6,426 and 66,242 females inmates in Federal and state prisons, respectively.
- More than 35.6% of jail inmates had committed their offense under the influence of drugs.

40

- An estimated $38 billion were spent on corrections in 1996, more than $30 billion was spent incarcerating individuals who had a history of drug and or alcohol abuse, were convicted of drug or alcohol violations, were using drugs or alcohol at the time of their crimes, or had committed their crimes to get money to buy drugs.
- The average cost per year to incarcerate an inmate in the United States is $20,674, the Federal average cost $23,542 and the State average is $20,261. Annual costs among local jail systems vary widely, from $8,037 to $66,795.
- Federal and State prisons house 1,254,577 inmates.
- Local jails house 596,485 inmates
- There are 712,713 people on parole
- 71,020 are on Federal parole
- 641,693 are on state parole
- 3,773,623 people are on probation
- There are 32,816 people on Federal probation
- 3,740,808 people are on state and local probation
- The total estimated correction population is 6,288,600 +
- Approximately 73% of local jails provide drug treatment or programs, with 32.1% providing detoxification, 29.6% providing drug education, and 63.7% providing self-help programs.
- About 61% of convicted jail inmates who committed their offenses under the influence of drugs or alcohol had received treatment in the past.
- For every $1 spent in treatment our society saved $3.

Marijuana: is a green, brown, or gray mixture of dried, shredded leaves, stems, seeds, and flowers of the hemp plant know as cannabis sativa. Cannabis is a term that refers to marijuana and other drugs made from the same plant. Other forms of cannabis include sinsemilla, hashish, and hash oil. All forms of cannabis are mind-altering (psychoactive) drugs.

The main active chemical in marijuana is THC (delta – 9 – tetrahydrocannabinol) Short term effects of marijuana use include; problems with memory and learning, distorted perception, difficulty in thinking and problem solving, loss of coordination, increased heart rate, and anxiety.

Marijuana is usually smoked as a cigarette (called a joint) or in a pipe or bong. Marijuana has also appeared in blunts, which are cigars that have been emptied of tobacco and refilled with marijuana, sometimes in combination with another drug, such as crack. It can also be mixed into foods or used to brew tea.

Extent of Use: According to the National Survey on Drugs and Health, of the 14.6 million past month marijuana users in 2002, about one third, or 4.8 million persons, used it on 20 or more days in the past month.

An estimated 40% of Americans aged 12 or older had used marijuana or hashish in their lifetime. There were an estimated 2.6 million new marijuana users in 2001.

A 2002 SAMHSA report, Initiation of Marijuana Use: Trends, Patterns and Implications, conclude that the younger children are when they first use marijuana, the more likely they are to use cocaine and heroin and become dependent on drugs as adults. The report found that 62% of adult's age 26 or older that used marijuana before they were 15 years old reported that they had used cocaine in their lifetime.

According to the 2003 Monitoring the Future Study, 17.5% of eighth graders, 34.4% of tenth graders, and 46.1% of twelfth graders had used marijuana in their lifetime.

Heath Effects: Marijuana abuse is associated with many detrimental health effects. These effects can include: frequent respiratory infections, impaired memory and learning, increased heart rate, anxiety and panic attacks. Marijuana meets the criteria for an addictive drug and animal studies suggest marijuana causes physical dependence and some people report withdraw symptoms.

Someone who smokes marijuana regularly may have many of the same respiratory problems that tobacco smokers do, such as daily cough and phlegm production, more frequent acute chest illnesses, a heightened risk of lung infections, and greater tendency toward obstructed airways. Cancer of the respiratory tract and lungs may also be promoted by marijuana smoke. Marijuana has the potential to promote cancer of the lungs and other parts of the respiratory track because marijuana smoke contains 50% to 70% more carcinogenic hydrocarbons than tobacco.

Marijuana's damage to short – term memory seems to occur because THC alters the way in which information is processed by the hippocampus, a brain area responsible for memory formation.

In one study, researchers compared marijuana smoking and non-smoking 12th graders' scores on standardized tests of verbal and mathematical skills. Although all of the students had scored equally well in 4th grade, those who were heavy marijuana smokers, i.e., those who used marijuana seven or more times per week, scored significantly lower in 12th grade than non-smokers. Another study of 129 college students found that among heavy users of marijuana critical skills related to attention, memory, and learning were significantly impaired, even after they had not used the drug for at least 24 hours.

- During 2002, marijuana was the second most frequently mentioned illicit drug reported to the Drug Abuse Warning Network (cocaine was the first) by emergency departments nationwide.
- There were 119,474 marijuana emergency departments mentions in 2001.
- Approximately 16% of marijuana emergency departments mentions in 2002 involved patients ages 6-17, 31% involved 18-25 years-old, 21% 26-34 years-old, and 32% involved individuals 35 years of age and older.
- Death investigation in 42 metropolitan areas across the United States. Cannabis ranked among the 10 most common drugs in 16 cities, including Detroit (74 death), Dallas (65 deaths), and Kansas City (63 deaths). Marijuana is very often reported in combination with other substances; in metropolitan areas that reported any marijuana in drug abuse deaths, an average of 79% of those deaths involved marijuana and at least one other substance.

43

Treatment: In 2000, there were 236,638 admissions to treatment facilities in the U.S., in which marijuana was the primary substance of abuse, accounting for 14.8% of the total admissions. Those admitted to treatment for marijuana in 2000 were primarily male (75.9%), white (56.6%), and young (46% under 20 years of age at admissions). Among those admitted to treatment for primary abuse of marijuana in 2000, approximately 56% had used the drug by age 14 and 91.9% had used the drug by the age of 18.

Arrest & Sentencing: In 2002, there were a total of 1,538,813 state and local arrest for drug abuse violations in the United States. Of the drug arrests, 5.4% were for marijuana sale and manufacturing and 39.9% were for marijuana possession.

- In 2001 the United States Sentencing Commission reported that there were 7,991 Federal drug offenders sentenced in U.S. Courts for marijuana – related offenses. The majority of these offenses were convictions for drug trafficking.
- There has been an increase of marijuana use among 18-20 year olds.
- Marijuana produced from Mexico remains the most widely available in the United States. However, domestically grown marijuana is still available.
- Canada is becoming a source country for indoor-grown, high-potency (15 to 25 percent THC) marijuana.
- 3,341,840 cultivated marijuana plants were eradicated in the United States during 2002. The five leading states for indoor growing activity were California, Washington, Texas, Floridian, and Michigan. Major outdoor growing states in 2002 include California, Tennessee, Hawaii, Kentucky, and North Carolina.
- U.S Federal authorities seized more than 2.4 million pounds of marijuana in 2002. This is down from 2.7 million pounds in 2001.
- Marijuana sellers are more likely to operate independently than as part of organized operations.

44

However, organizations with varying degrees of structure do exist.

- According to National Survey on Drug Use and Health most marijuana users (56.7%) got the drug for free or shared someone else's marijuana in 2002.
- More than half (55.9%) of marijuana smokers purchased it outside the home, apartment, or dorm.
- Almost 9% of youths who bought their marijuana obtained it outside a school building, and 4.8% bought it outside of school property.

Marijuana Street Terms

Term - 420 - definition - Marijuana use
Term - B C bud - definition - High-grade marijuana from Canada
Term - Bud - definition - Marijuana
Term - Chronic - definition - Marijuana
Term - Dope - definition - Marijuana
Term - Ganja - definition - Marijuana from Jamaica
Term - Herb - definition - Marijuana
Term - Homegrown - definition - Marijuana
Term - Hydro - definition - Marijuana grown in water (hydroponic)
Term - Indo - definition - Marijuana from Northern Ca.
Term - Mary Jane - definition - Marijuana
Term - Shake - definition - Marijuana
Term - Sinsemilla - definition - Potent Marijuana

Cocaine: Pure cocaine was first used in the early 1880's as a local anesthetic in eye, nose, and throat surgeries because of its ability to provide anesthesia was well as to constrict blood vessels and limit bleeding. Many of its therapeutic applications are now obsolete due to the development of safer drugs.

Cocaine is the most potent stimulant of natural origin. This substance can be snorted, smoked, or injected. When snorted, cocaine powder is inhaled through the nose where it is absorbed into the bloodstream through nasal tissues. When injected, the user uses a needle to release the drug directly into the bloodstream. Smoking involves inhaling cocaine vapor or smoke into the lungs where absorption into the bloodstream is as rapid as by injection. Each of these methods of administration poses great risk to the user.

Crack is cocaine that has been processed from cocaine hydrochloride to a free base for smoking. Crack cocaine is processed with ammonia or sodium bicarbonate (baking soda) and water. It is then heated to remove the hydrochloride producing a form of cocaine that can be smoked.

Extent of Use: During 2001, there were approximately 1,160,000 new cocaine users in the United States. The average age of these who first used cocaine during the year was 20.8 years. According to the 2002 National Survey on Drug Use and Health, approximately 33.9 million Americans ages 12 and older had tried cocaine at least once in their lifetime, representing 14.4% of the population ages 12 and older. Approximately 5.9 million (2.5%) has used cocaine in the past year and 2.0 million (0.9%) has used cocaine within the past month.

- Among high school students surveyed as part of the 2003 Monitoring the Future Study, 3.6% of eighth graders, 5.1% of tenth graders, and 7.7% of twelfth graders reported using cocaine at least once during their lifetimes.
- Students reporting trying cocaine once or twice; eighth graders 48.7%, tenth graders 57.6%, and twelfth graders 47.3%.
- Students using crack occasionally; eighth graders 70.3%, tenth graders 76.4%, and twelfth graders 64.0%.
- Students trying cocaine in powder form once or twice; eighth graders 43.7%, tenth graders 51.8%, and twelfth graders 46.2%.
- Students using cocaine powder occasionally; eighth graders 65.8%, tenth graders 71.4%, and twelfth graders 82.3%.

- During 2002, 8.2% of college students and 13.5% of young adults ages (19-28) reported using cocaine at least once during their lifetimes.
- Approximately 4.8% of college students and 5.8% of young adults reported past year use of cocaine, and 1.6% of college students and 2.2% of young adults reported past moth use of cocaine.
- According to preliminary data from the Arrestee Drug Abuse Monitoring (ADAM) Program, 30.4% of adult male arrestees and 30.7% of female's arrestees tested positive for cocaine at the time of their arrest in 2002.
- Crack-Cocaine used in past 7 days by males 12.2%, by females 18.2%; in powder cocaine males 6.3% in females 6.1%
- Crack-Cocaine use in the past 30 days by males 14.4% by females 19.8%; in powder cocaine 8.9% for males and 8.3% by females.
- Crack-Cocaine used in the past year by males 18.3%, by females 26.2%; in powder cocaine 13.9% for males and 12.0% for females.
- Avg.# of days used in the past 30 days for crack-cocaine for males was 7.8 days for females 10.7 days; for powder cocaine, males 4.1 days and for females also 4.1 days.

Health Effects: Cocaine is a strong central nervous system stimulant. Physical effects of cocaine use include constricted blood vessels and increased temperature, heart rate, and blood pressure. Users may also experiences feelings of restlessness, irritability, and anxiety.

Evidence suggests that users who smoke or inject cocaine may be at even greater risk of causing harm to themselves than those who snort the substance. For example, cocaine smokers also form acute respiratory problems including coughing, shortness of breath, and severe chest pains with lung trauma and bleeding. A user who injects cocaine is at risk of transmitting or acquiring diseases if needles or other injection equipment are shared.

- Cocaine is a powerfully addictive drug and compulsive cocaine use seems to develop more rapidly when the substance is smoked rather than snorted.
- A tolerance to the cocaine high may be developed and many addicts report that they fail to achieve as much pleasure as they did from their first cocaine exposure.
- Smoking crack delivers large quantities of the drug to the lungs, producing effects comparable to intravenous injection.
- The effects of smoking crack-cocaine are felt almost immediately after smoking, are very intense, but do not last long.
- The high from smoking cocaine may last 5 to 10 minutes.
- The high from snorting cocaine can last for 15 to 20 minutes.
- Cocaine use has increased 47% since 1995.
- The average age of those admitted to treatment for cocaine in 2001 was 36.3 years for smoking cocaine user and 34.2 years for non-smoked cocaine users.
- 40% of the total arrest made by the DEA in 2002 were for cocaine-related.

Production and Trafficking: Cocaine is extracted from the leaves of the coca plant, which is indigenous to the Andean highlands of South America. During 2000, the majority (approximately 75%) of Andean coca was grown in Colombia, with Peru and Bolivia ranking second and third.

The United States and the Mexico border is the primary point of entry for cocaine shipments being smuggled into the United States. Sources indicate that approximately 65% of the cocaine entering the U.S. crosses the Southwest border.

Cocaine is usually sold in grams and "eight balls" (1/8 ounce). $100 per gram is the going price for powder cocaine; crack tends to be sold in 0.1 and 0.2 gram rocks, which sell generally for $10 and $20.

Powder cocaine and crack cocaine are being sold in central city areas. Suburban areas are also frequently mentioned as areas for powder cocaine.

- In some cities cocaine has been mixed with caffeine, chalk, laundry detergent, rat poison, meat tenderizer, baby laxatives, and talcum and baby powder before it was sold to the use.
- Federal agents seized 225,122 pounds of cocaine under Federal-wide Seizure System (FDSS).
- Cocaine was first Federally-regulated in December of 1941 with the passage of the Harrison Act. This Act banned non-medical use of cocaine; prohibited importation; imposed the same criminal penalties for cocaine users as for opium, morphine and heroin users; and required a strict accounting of medical prescriptions for cocaine.
- Cocaine was classified as a Schedule II substance in 1970. Schedule II substances have a high potential for abuse, a currently accepted medical use in treatment in the U.S. with severe restrictions, and may lead to severe psychological or physical dependence.
- Cocaine can currently be administered by a doctor for legitimate medical use such as anesthetic for some eye, ear, and throat surgeries.

Street Terms For Cocaine

Term "Blow" Definition - cocaine
Term "Horn" Definition - to inhale cocaine
Term "Nose candy" Definition - cocaine
Term "Snowball" Definition - cocaine and heroin
Term "Binger" Definition - crack addicts
Term "Ooilies" Definition - marijuana laced with crack
Term "Tornado" Definition - crack
Term "Wicky stick" Definition - PCP,
        marijuana and crack

Crack Cocaine: The term "crack" refers to the cracking sound heard when the substances is heated, presumably from the sodium bicarbonate that is used in the production of crack. Crack became enormously popular in the mid-1980's due in part to its almost immediate high and the fact that it is inexpensive to produce and buy.

Crack is a highly addictive form of cocaine that is typically smoked. While nearly always smoked, there are reports of users injecting crack in Baltimore, Boston, Sioux Falls, and Washington D.C.

Extent of Use: According to the 2002 National Survey on Drug Use and Health, approximately 8.4 million Americans ages 12 and older reported trying crack at least once during their lifetime. Approximately 1.6 million (0.7%) reported past year crack cocaine use and 567,000 (0.2%) reported past month crack use. Among high school students surveyed as part of the 2003 Monitoring the Future Study, 2.5% of eighth graders, 2.7% of tenth graders, and 3.6% of twelfth graders reported using crack cocaine at least once during their lifetimes.

Percent of students reporting crack cocaine use in 2003

- Use of crack in the past month, eighth graders reported use 0.7%, tenth graders reported use 0.7% and twelfth graders reported use 0.9%.
- Use of crack in the past year, 1.6% of eighth graders reported that they used crack in the last year; 1.6% of tenth graders also reported that they had used crack in the past year; and 2.2% twelfth graders reported using crack in the past year.
- Lifetime use of crack, 2.5% of eighth graders reported that they had use crack in their lifetime, 2.7% of tenth graders reported that they had used crack cocaine in their lifetime, and 3.6% of twelfth graders reported using crack cocaine in their lifetime.
- Regarding the ease by which one can obtain crack cocaine; 22.5% of eight graders, 29.6% of tenth graders,

and 35.3% of twelfth graders surveyed in 2003 reported that crack cocaine was fairly easy or very easy to obtain.

- Nearly 49% of eighth graders, 58% of tenth graders, and 47% of twelfth graders reported that using crack cocaine once or twice was a "great risk".
- 48.7% of eighth graders report using crack once or twice.
- 57.6% of tenth graders report using crack once or twice.
- 47.3% of twelfth graders report using crack cocaine once or twice.
- 70.3% of eighth graders report using crack occasionally.
- 76.4% of tenth graders report using crack occasionally.
- 64.0% of twelfth graders reported using crack occasionally.

Health Effects: Evidence suggests that users who smoke or inject cocaine may be at even greater risk of causing harm to themselves than those who snort the substances. Cocaine smokers may suffer from acute respiratory problems including coughing, shortness of breath, and severe chest pains with lung trauma and bleeding. Smoking crack cocaine can also cause particularly aggressive paranoid behavior in users.

An added danger of cocaine use is when cocaine and alcohol are consumed at the same time. When these substances are mixed, the human liver combines cocaine and alcohol and manufactures a third substance, coca-ethy-lene. This intensifies cocaine's euphoric effects, while also possibly increasing the risk of sudden death. Most cocaine related deaths are a result of cardiac arrest or seizures followed by respiratory arrest.

Cocaine is a powerfully addictive drug. Compulsive cocaine users seems to develop more rapidly when the substances is smoked rather than snorted. A tolerances to the cocaine high may be developed and many addicts report that they fail to achieve as much pleasure as they did from their first cocaine exposure.

During 2002, emergency departments nationwide reported 42,146 mentions to the Drug Abuse Warning Network.

Smoking crack delivers large quantities of the drug to the lungs, producing effects comparable to intravenous injection. These effects are felt almost immediately after smoking, are very

51

intense, but do not last for long. The high from smoking crack cocaine may last from 5 to 10 minutes, while the high from snorting the drug can last for 15 to 20 minutes.

Cocaine is a strong central nervous system stimulant. Physical effects of cocaine use, including crack, include constricted blood vessels and increased temperature, heart rate, and blood pressure. Users may also experience feelings of restlessness, irritability and anxiety.

Common Terms Associated with Crack

Term "Bingers" Definition - crack addicts
Term "Geeker" Definition - crack user
Term "Jelly Beans" Definition - crack
Term "Moon-rock" Definition - crack mixed with heroin
Term "Oolies" Definition - marijuana laced with crack
Term "Rooster" Definition - crack
Term "Tornado" Definition - crack
Term "Wicky Stick" Definition - PCP, marijuana,
    and crack

Inhalants: The term inhalants refers to more than a thousand different household and commercial products that can be intentionally abused by sniffing or huffing (inhaling through one's mouth) for an intoxicating effect. These products are composed of volatile solvents and substances commonly found in commercial adhesives, lighter fluid, cleaning solutions, gasoline, paint, and glue and paint products. Easy accessibility, low cost, and easy to conceal make inhalants, for many, one of the first substances abused.

According to the National Survey on Drug and Health there were an estimated 1,125,000 new inhalant users in 2001, up from 86,000 in 1995. In 2002, of those surveyed aged 12 and older, 22,870,000 reported using an inhalant at least once in their lifetime. Typically, the first use of inhalants occurs between late childhood and early adolescence.

According to the Monitoring The Future Study, during 2003, 11.2% of 12th graders, 12.7% of 10th graders, and 15.8% of 8th graders have used an inhalant in their lifetime.

Percent of Students Reporting Inhalant Use in 2003

Student inhalant use in the past month for 8th graders was 4.1%, for 10th graders it was 2.2%, and for 12th graders it was 1.5%.

Student inhalant use in the past year for 8th graders was 8.7%, for 10th graders is was 5.4%, and for 12th graders it was 3.9%.

Student inhalant use in their lifetime, for 8th graders it was 15.8%, for 10th graders it was 12.7%, and for 12th graders it was 11.2%.

- When asked about the degree of risk associated with inhalants, 42.8% of 8th graders and 48.7% of 10th graders reported feeling that using inhalants once or twice a week was a "great risk".
- In 2002, 86.1% of the 8th graders and 86.6% of the 10th graders disapproved of people who try inhalants once or twice a week. In addition, 90.4% of 8th graders and 91.8% of 10th graders disapprove of using inhalants regularly.
- Among college students surveyed during 2002, 7.7% reported using inhalants during their lifetime.
- According to the Center of Disease Control and Prevention's 2001 Youth Risk Behavior Surveillance Survey (YRBSS), 14.7% of high school students surveyed nationwide had used an inhalant during their lifetime; 14.9% were females and 14.5% were males.

Health Effects: While different in composition, most abused inhalants produced effects similar to an anesthetic, which slows the body functions. Inhalants cause intoxicating effects when administered via the nose or mouth into the lungs in sufficient quantities. If taken repeatedly, intoxication may last a few minutes to several hours. At first, users may feel slightly stimulated with successive inhalations, they may feel less inhibited and less in control. Finally, a user can lose consciousness.

Sniffing highly concentrated amounts of chemicals in solvents or aerosol sprays can cause heart failure or death, especially when abuse of flu-or-o-carbons or butane-type gases is involved. In addition, high concentrations of inhalants can lead to the displacement of oxygen in the lungs and central nervous system resulting in death by suffocation.

Permanent effects caused by the use of inhalants include healing loss, peripheral neuropathies or limb spasms, central nervous system or brain damage, and bone marrow damage. Additional serious side effects include; liver and kidney damage as well as blood oxygen depletion.

The number of emergency department mentions involving inhalants decreased from 1,141 mentions in 2000 to 522 mentions in 2001. However, in 2002 the emergency department mentions increased to 1,496 for the use of inhalants.

- In 2002, there were 1,234 admissions to treatment facilities in which inhalants were the primary substance of abuse.
- Inhalant admissions were primarily male (73%) white (71%), and young (46% under 20 years old).
- Those admitted to treatment for primary inhalants use began at an early age; 27% used inhalants by the age of 12, and another 28% used inhalants by the age of 14.
- According to the 1997 Bureau of Justice Statistics Survey of Inmates in Adult State and Federal Correctional Facilities, 7.7% of Federal prisoners had tried inhalants in their lifetime, 2.6% reported using inhalants regularly, and .05% reported using inhalants in the month before committing their offense. Among State prisoners, 14.4% had tried inhalants in their lifetime, 5.4% reported using inhalants regularly, and 1% reported using inhalants in the month before committing their offense.
- Although not regulated under the Controlled Substance Act, many State legislatures have attempted to deter

youth who buy legal products to get high by placing restrictions on the sale of these products to minors.

- As reported by the National Conference of State Legislatures, by 2000, 38 States had adopted laws preventing the sale, use, and/or distribution to minors of various products commonly abused as inhalants. Some states have introduced fines, incarceration, or mandatory treatment for the sale, distribution, use, and/or possession of inhalable chemicals.

Common Terms Associated with inhalants

Term "Air Blast" Definition - inhalants
Term "Buzz Bomb" Definition - Nitrous Oxide
Term "Glading" Definition - using inhalants
Term "Huffer" Definition - inhalants abuser
Term "Bagging" Definition - using inhalants
Term "Climax" Definition - using inhalants
Term "Gluey" Definition - sniffing or inhaling glue
Term "Poor Man's Pot" Definition - inhalants

LSD: Commonly know as "acid", was discovered in 1938 when a chemist working for Sandoz Laboratories in Switzerland synthesized the drug. It was developed initially as a circulatory and respiratory stimulant. In the 1940's, interest in the drug was revived when it was thought to be a possible treatment for schizophrenia. During the 1960's, the first group of casual LSD users evolved and expanded into a subculture.

LSD (lysergic acid diethylamide) is manufactured from lysergic acid, which is found in ergot, a fungus that grows on rye and other grains. It is sold on the street in tablets, capsules, and occasionally, in liquid form. LSD is an odorless and colorless substance which has a slightly bitter taste and is usually ingested orally. It is often added to absorbent paper, such as blotter paper, and divided into small-decorated squares, with each square representing one dose.

The Drug Enforcement Administration (DEA) reports that the strength of LSD samples obtained currently from illicit sources rang from 20 to 80 millionths of a gram (micrograms) of LSD per dose. This is much less than the levels reported during the 1960's and early 1970's, when the dosage ranged from 100 to 200 micrograms or higher per unit. **Generally**, the dosage level that will produce a hallucinogenic effect in humans is 25 micrograms.

Extent of Use: According to the National Survey on Drug Use and Health, 112,000 Americans 12 years and older were current LSD users during 2002. Of those surveyed, 10.4% indicated using LSD at least once in their lifetime. Almost 3% of those surveyed between the ages of 12 and 17 (2.7%) reported the use of LSD at least once in their lifetime, where as 15.9% of those surveyed between the age of 18 and 25 reported lifetime LSD use.

Percentage of High School Students
Reporting LSD Use in 2003

- 8th graders reported lifetime use at 2.1%, annual use at 1.3%, and last 30 days 0.6%
- 10th graders reported lifetime use at 3.5%, annual use at 1.7% and last 30 days 0.6%
- 12th graders reported lifetime use at 5.9%, annual use at 1.9% and last 30 days 0.6%

Percent of Collage Students and Young Adults
Reporting LSD use in 2002

College students reported a lifetime use at 8.6%, annual use at 2.1%, and last 30 days 0.2%

Young adults reported a lifetime use at 15.1%, annual use at 1.8%, and last 30days 0.3%

Health Effects: LSD, although commonly perceived as harmless, can lead to many consequences for users. Powerful hallucinations can lead to acute panic reactions when the mental effects of LSD cannot be controlled and when the user wishes to end the drug-induced state.

- The mental effects of LSD use can cause psychotic crises and add to existing psychiatric problems
- The effects of LSD are unpredictable
- Users feel the first effects of the drug within 30 to 90 minutes of ingestion
- The experiences last for extended periods of time and typically begin to clear after 12 hours
- The physical effects include dilated pupils, higher body temperature, sleeplessness, dry mouth, and tremors.
- If taken in a large enough dose the drug produces delusions and visual hallucinations.
- The user's sense of time and self changes, sensations may seem to cross-over giving the user the feeling of hearing colors and seeing sounds. These changes can be frightening and can cause panic.
- Many LSD users experience flashbacks, recurrences of certain aspects of the person's experience, without the user having taken the drug again.
- A flashback occurs suddenly, often without warning, and may occur within a few days or more than a year after LSD is used.
- LSD users may manifest relatively long-lasting psychoses, such as schizophrenia or sever depression.
- Most LSD users voluntarily decrease or stop using the drug over time.
- LSD is not considered an addictive drug since it does not produce compulsive drug-seeking behavior, as do cocaine, amphetamine, heroin, alcohol, and nicotine.
- LSD produces tolerance, so some users who take the drug repeatedly must take progressively higher doses to achieve the state of intoxication that they had previously achieved.
- Death related to LSD abuse has occurred as a result of the panic reactions, hallucination, delusions, and paranoia experienced by users.

- The cause of most LSD-related problems is the intense visual illusions that seem real and become overpowering, prompting the user to want to withdraw from the drug state immediately.
- At low dosage levels, the visual images are intensified and color or flashes of light are seen. The visual images progress to brightly colored geometric designs and become distorted.
- At higher dosages, images appear as distortions of reality or as completely new visual images and can be seen with the eyes open or closed.
- Hallucinations can also take other forms; thoughts become dreamlike or free flowing, perception of time can become slowed or distorted, and out-of-body experiences or the perception that one's body has merged with another person or object may also occur.
- In 2002 there were 819 mentions of LSD in emergency departments. This was a decrease from the 5,682 LSD mentions in 1995.
- During 2002, the age group in which LSD was most frequently mentioned was 18-25 years of age at 506 mentions.
- The race / ethnic groups and gender accounting for the most LSD mentions was; white with 670 mentions and male with 776 mentions. More than 300 of those going to the ER because of LSD where there because of an unexpected reaction to the drug.

Reason for
LSD-Related Emergency Department Contact in 2002

Reason - unexpected reaction, number of visits - 349
Reason - overdose, number of visits - 147
Reason - seeking detoxification, number of visits - 119
Reason - accident or injury, number of visits - 8
Reason - other visits - 44

Reason for LSD use as Reported by LSD – Related Emergency Department Contacts in 2002

Reason - Psychic effects number of visits - 421
Reason - Dependence, number of visits - 352
Reason - suicide, number of visits - 49
Reason - unknown motive for drug use, number of visits - 65

Production and Trafficking:

LSD is available in retail quantities in almost every state. Since the 1960's LSD has been manufactured illegally within the United States. It is reportedly produced on the West Coast, particularly in San Francisco, Northern California, the Pacific Northwest, and recently the Midwest.

The production of LSD is a time-consuming and complex procedure that requires a high degree of chemical experts. There have been few LSD laboratories seized in the United States because of infrequent and irregular production cycles. Chemists do not usually sell the drug, but instead distribute it to trusted associates.

- LSD is produced in a crystal form that is converted to liquid and distributed primarily in form of squares of blotter paper saturated with the liquid.
- Distribution of LSD is unique within the drug culture.
- An abundance of mail order sales has created a marketplace for sellers to remain virtually unknown to the buyers, which gives the drug traffickers a level of protection from drug law enforcement.
- Rock concerts continue to be favorite distribution sites for LSD traffickers. However, distribution at raves throughout the United States is becoming more popular.
- LSD is relatively inexpensive.
- The average price is about $5 per dosage unit and less than $1 per dose unit in wholesale lots of 1,000 or more.
- Pure, high-potency LSD is a clear or white, odorless crystalline material that is soluble in water.

- Variations or by-products can cause LSD to range in color from clear or white, to tan or black.
- To mask the product, distributors often apply LSD to off-white, tan, or yellow paper to disguise discoloration.
- LSD is a Schedule 1 substance, meaning it has a high potential for abuse; there is no currently accepted medical use in treatment in the United States.

Street Terms

Term "Acid", definition LSD
Term "Acid cube", definition sugar cube containing LSD
Term "Black Breaker", definition LSD
Term "Battery Acid", definition LSD
Term "Candy-flipping", definition combining LSD and MDMA (ecstasy)
Term "Come Home" definition end a LSD trip
Term "Dots", definition LSD
Term "Elvis" definition LSD
Term "Flash" definition LSD with cocaine injected
Term "Loony Toons" definition LSD
Term "Lucky in the sky with diamonds" definition LSD
Term "Outer Limits", definition crack and LSD
Term "Pane" definition LSD
Term "Trails" definition LSD induced perception of moving objects with trails behind them.

OxyContin: OxyContin is a prescription painkiller used to control mild to moderate pain, chronic pain, and pain related to cancer and other debilitating conditions. OxyContin contains, Oxycodone, the medication's active ingredient, in a timed-released tablet. Oxycodone products have been illicitly abused for the past 30 years.

OxyContin produces opiate-like effects and is sometimes used as a substitute for heroin. Illicit users of OxyContin include crushing the tablet and ingesting or smoking it. Most individuals who abuse this drug do so to avoid withdraw symptoms. Those who take the drug repeatedly can develop a tolerance or resistance to the drug's effects.

According to the National Survey on Drug Use and Health, approximately 1.9 million persons age 12 or older had used OxyContin non-medically at least once in their lifetime during 2002.

A questionnaire about OxyContin was included in the 2002 Monitoring the Future Study for the first time. During 2002, 1.3% of 8th graders, 3.0% of 10th graders, and 4.0% of 12th graders reported using OxyContin within the past year. During 2003, 1.7% of 8th graders, 3.6% of 10th graders, and 4.5% of 12th graders reported using OxyContin within the past year.

According to the November 2002 Pulse Check: Trends in Drug Abuse, OxyContin diversions and abuse were reported as emerging in 13 of the 20 Pulse Check sites, including; Baltimore, MD; Billings, MT; Boston, MA; Chicago, IL; Columbia, SC; Denver, CO; Detroit, MI; Memphis, TN: Miami, FL; New Orleans, LA; Philadelphia, PA; Portland, OR; and Seattle, WA.

Health Effects: Most individuals who are prescribed OxyContin will not become addicted, although they may become dependent on the drug and will experience withdraw symptoms when use is stopped.

According to the Drug Use Warning Network (DAWN) emergency department data, there was a 107% increase in the number of Oxycodone combination mentions from 2000 – 2002.

During 2002, there were 22,397 mentions of Oxycodone combinations, compared to the 10,825 mentions during 2000.

Emergency Department Mentions of Oxycodone 1996-2002

1996 Combination Mentions 3,190;
Single Entity Mentions 100
1997 Combination Mentions 5,012;
Single Entity Mentions 372
1998 Combination Mentions 5,211;
Single Entity Mentions 1,034

1999 Combination Mentions 6,429;
   Single Entity Mentions 1,804
2000 Combination Mentions 10,825;
   Single Entity Mentions 3,792
2001 Combination Mentions 18,409;
   Single Entity Mentions 11,100
2002 Combination Mentions 22,397;
   Single Entity Mentions 14,996

- According to the Drug Abuse Warning Network (DAWN) mortality data, Oxycodone ranked among the most common drugs in 19 cities, Baltimore was tied for second with 34 mentions behind Philadelphia who had 88 mentions.
- As of November 1, 2002, medical examiner offices in 31 States reported 1,096 overdose death involving Oxycodone, 117 of which were related to OxyContin.
- OxyContin is the primary drug of abuse among substantial percentage of clients in several treatment programs in Pulse Check Cities.
- During 2001 Oxycodone was reported in 1,039 admissions as the primary substance of abuse.
- Many abusers of OxyContin will travel from doctor to doctor to get a prescription for the controlled substance.
- Some doctors who have improper prescribing practices will give prescriptions for OxyContin to their patients.
- Crime related sales of OxyContin are usually non-violent, although, violent crimes were reported in Boston, Honolulu, Los Angeles, and Portland relating to OxyContin sales.
- According to the Drug Enforcement Administration, during 2000, there were 432 OxyContin theft and loss incidents, with the majority of incidents from employee pilferage. OxyContin thefts and loss incidents increased to 905 during 2002, with the majority of incidents from night break-ins, armed robberies, and employee pilferage. As of June 2003, there were 399 OxyContin theft and loss incidents.

OxyContin Theft and Loss Incidents, January 2000 Through June 2003

Type of Incident and the Year
Night Break – Ins
2000 –176
2001 –204
2002 –206
2003 –121
Total number of incidents 707

Armed Robberies
2000 – 43
2001 – 204
2002 – 277
2003 – 107
Total number of incidents 631

Employee Pilferage
2000 – 119
2001 – 217
2002 – 273
2003 – 95
Total number of incidents 704

Customer Theft
2000 –15
2001 –20
2002 –28
2003 –24
Total number of incidents 87

Lost in Transit
2000 –79
2001 –113
2002 –121

2003 –52
Total number of incidents 365
Total number for all types of incidents 2,494

OxyContin Loss by Dosage Units,
January 2000 Through June 2003

Year   Dosage Units Lost
2000 – 218,339
2001 – 439,425
2002 – 506,711
2003 – 205,192 * Half year data
Total amount of dosage units of OxyContin loss in 3 ½ years was
1,369,667

- Oxycodone is a Schedule ll drug under the Controlled Substance Act. Schedule ll substances have a high potential for abuse.
- Many States have launched efforts to curb the illegal use of OxyContin; Maryland is NOT on that list. However, Maryland may be on the list of States working to establish legislation and prescription monitoring programs to deal with diverted pharmaceuticals?

Common Terms Associated with OxyContin

Term "40" Definition OxyContin
Term "80" Definition OxyContin
Term "Blue" Definition OxyContin
Term "Doctor Shopping" Definition obtaining pharmaceutical prescriptions from various doctors
Term "Hillbilly Heroin" Definition OxyContin
Term "Kicker" Definition OxyContin
Term "Oxy" Definition OxyContin
Term "Oxycotton" Definition OxyContin
Term "Pharming" Definition-consuming mix of prescription drugs

Steroids: Currently, there are more than 100 different types of anabolic steroids that have been developed; each requires a prescription to be used legally in the United States.

Anabolic steroids can be taken orally, injected intramuscularly, or rubbed on the skin when in form of gel or cream. These drugs are often used in patterns called cycling, which involve taking multiple doses of steroids over a specific period of time, stopping for a period, and starting again. Users also frequently combine several different types of steroids in a process know as stacking. By doing this, users believe that the different steroids will interact to produce an effect on muscle size.

Another mode of steroid is "pyramiding". This is a process in which users slowly escalate steroids use (increasing the number of drugs used at one time and/or the dose and frequency of one or more steroids) reaching a peak amount at mid-cycle and gradually tapering the dose toward the end of the cycle.

Extent of Use: Results from the 2003 Monitoring the Future Study, which surveys students in 8th, 10th, and 12th grades, show that 2.5% of 8th graders, 3.0% of 10th graders, and 3.5% of 12th graders reported using steroids at least once in their lifetime.

- 21.7% of 8th graders, 30.6% of 10th graders, and 40.7% of 12th graders surveyed in 2003 reported steroids were "fairly easy" or "very easy" to obtain.
- 55% of 12th graders surveyed in 2003 reported that using steroids was a "great risk".
- 5% of all high school students surveyed by the Centers of Disease Control and Prevention in 2001 reported lifetime use of steroid pills/shots without a doctor's prescription.
- 5.8% of 9th graders, 4.9% of 10th graders, 4.3% of eleventh graders, and 4.3% of 12th graders reported lifetime illegal use of steroids.
- During 2002, 1.6% of young adults (ages19-28) reported using steroids at least once during their lifetime.
- 0.4% of young adults (ages 19-28) reported past year steroid use, and 0.1% reported past month steroid use.

Health Effects: Anabolic steroid abuse has been associated with a wide range of adverse side effects ranging from some that are physically unattractive, such as acne and breast development in men, to others that are life threatening. Most of the effects are reversible if the abuser stops taking the drug, but some can be permanent. In addition to the physical effects, anabolic steroids can also cause increased irritability and aggression.

Some of the health consequences that can occur in both males and females include liver cancer, heart attacks, and elevated cholesterol levels. In addition to this, steroid use among adolescents may prematurely stop the lengthening of bones resulting in stunted growth.

- People who inject steroids also run the risk of contacting or transmitting hepatitis or HIV.
- Some steroid abusers experience withdrawal symptoms when they stop taking the drug.
- These withdrawal symptoms include mood swings, fatigue, restlessness, loss of appetite, insomnia, reduced sex drive, and depression.
- The depression can also lead to suicide attempts, and if left untreated, can persist for a year or more after the abuser stops taking the drug.
- Illicit anabolic steroids are often sold at gyms, competitions, and through mail operations after being smuggled into this country.
- Steroids are also illegally diverted from U.S. pharmacies or synthesized in clandestine laboratories.

Street Slang For Steroids
Arnolds
Gym Candy
Juice
Pumpers
Stackers
Weight Trainers

Club Drugs: In recent year, certain drugs have emerged and become popular among teen and young adults at dance clubs and "raves". These drugs include collectively termed "club drugs" include MDMA / Ecstasy (meth-ylene-dioxy-meth-am-phet-a-mine).

Producing both stimulant and psychedelic effects, MDMA is often used at parties because it enables party-goers to dance and remain active for a long period of time. This substance is usually ingested in tablet form, but can also be crushed and smoked, injected, or used in suppository form.

Rohypnol and GHB are often used in the commission of sexual assaults due to their ability to sedate and intoxicate unsuspected victims. Rohypnol (flunitrazepam), a sedative / tranquilizer, is legally available for prescription in over 50 countries outside of the United States and is widely available in Mexico, Colombia, and Europe. Although usually taken orally in pill form, reports have shown that users grind Rohypnol into a powder and snort the drug.

GHB (gamma hydroxybutyrate), available in an odorless, colorless liquid form or as a white powder material, is taken orally, and is frequently combined with alcohol. In addition to being used to incapacitate individuals for the commission of sexual assault / rape, GHB is also sometimes used by body builders for its alleged anabolic effects.

The abuse of ketamine (ketamine hydrochloride), a tranquilizer most often used on animals, became popular in the 1980's when it was realized that large doses cause reactions similar to those associated with the use of PCP, such as dream-like states and hallucinations. The liquid form of Ketamine can be injected, consumed in drinks, or added to smoke materials. The powder form can also be added to drinks, smoked, or dissolved and then injected. In some cases, katemine is being injected intramuscularly.

Extent of Use: According to the 2002 National Survey on Drug Use and Health, an estimated 10.2 million Americans aged 12 or older tried MDMA (Ecstasy) at least once in their lifetime, representing 4.3% of the United States population in that age group.

According to the 2003 Monitoring the Future Study, **3**.2% of 8th graders, 5.4% of 10th graders, and 8.3% of 12th graders reported using Ecstasy at least once during their lifetime.

- One percent of 8th graders and 10th graders reported using Rohypoln at least once during their lifetime. 12th grade data is not available. Lifetime use of GHB and katamine was not captured in the survey.

Percent of Students Reporting
Ecstasy and Rohypnol Use in 2003

8th graders use of Ecstasy 0.7%,
  use of Rohypnol 0.1% in the past month
8th graders use of Ecstasy 2.1%,
  use of Rohypnol 0.5% in the past year
8th graders use of Ecstasy 3.2%,
  use of Rohypnol 1.0% lifetime use
10th graders use of Ecstasy 1.1%,
  use of Rohypnol 0.2% in the past month
10th graders use of Ecstasy 3.0%,
  use of Rohypnol 0.6% in the last year
10th graders use of Ecstasy 5.4%,
  use of Rohypnol 1.0% lifetime use
12th graders use of Ecstasy 1.3%,
  in the past month, use of Rohypnol data not available
12th graders use of Ecstasy 4.5%,
  use of Rohypnol 1.3% in the past year
12th graders use of Ecstasy 8.3% lifetime use,
  use of Rohypnol for lifetime not available

- Data showing past year use of GHB and katamine are captured in the Monitoring the Future Study, in 2003, 0.9% of 8th graders, 1.4% of 10th graders, and 1.4% of twelfth graders reported using GHB at least once in the past year.
- Approximately 42% of 8th graders and nearly 50% of 10th graders surveyed in 2003 reported that using Ecstasy once or twice was a great risk.

- College students lifetime use of Ecstasy is 12.7% reported in 2002
- Young adults lifetime use of Ecstasy 14.6% reported in 2002

Health Effects: Using Ecstasy can cause serious psychological and physical damage. The possible psychological effects include confusion, depression, anxiety, and paranoia and may last for weeks after ingesting the substance.

Physically, a user may experience nausea, faintness, and significant increase in heart rate and blood pressure. Ecstasy use can cause hyperthermia (unusually high body temperature), muscle breakdown, seizures, stroke, kidney and cardiovascular system failure, and may lead to death. Also, chronic use of Ecstasy has been found to produce long-lasting, possibly permanent, damage to the sections of the brain critical to thought and memory.

Rohypnol, GHB, and ketamine are all central nervous system depressants. Lower doses of Rohypnol can cause mussel relaxation and can produce general sedative and hypnotic effects. In higher doses, Rohypnol causes a loss of muscle control, loss of consciousness, and partial amnesia. When combined with alcohol, the toxic effects of Rohypnol can be aggravated. The sedative effects of Rohypnol begin to appear approximately 15-20 minutes after the drug is ingested. The effects typically last for 4-6 hours after administration of the drug, but some cases have been reported in which the effects were experienced 12 or more hours after administration.

GHB has been shown to produce drowsiness, nausea, unconsciousness, seizers, severe respiratory depression, and coma. Additionally, GHB has increasingly become involved in poisoning, overdoses, date rapes, and fatalities.

The use of ketamine produces effects similar to PCP and LSD, causing distorted perceptions of sight and sound and making the user feel disconnected and out of control.

The overt hallucinatory effects of ketamine are relatively short acting, lasting approximately one hour or less. However, the users senses, judgment, and coordination may be affected for up to 24 hours after the initial use of the drug. Use of this drug can also bring about respiratory depression, heart rate abnormalities, and withdraw syndrome.

- The number of emergency department Ecstasy mentions reported to the Drug Abuse Warning Network (DAWN) has increased from 421 in 1995, to 4,026 in 2002. During this same time period, the number of GHB mentions increased from 145 to 3,330. The number of ketamine mentions has increased from 81 in 1996, to 260 in 2002.
- In response to the Ecstasy Anti-Proliferation Act of 2002, the United States Sentencing Commission increased the guideline sentence for trafficking Ecstasy (MDMA). The new amendment, enacted on November 1, 2001, increases the sentence from trafficking 800 MDMA pills by 300%, from 15 months to 5 years.

It also increases the penalty for trafficking 8,000 pills by nearly 200%, from 41 months to 10 years.

- MDMA is primarily manufactured in clandestine laboratories located in Europe, particularly the Netherlands and Belgium. From these labs, MDMA is transported to the U.S. and other countries using a variety of means, including commercial airlines, express mail services, and sea cargo. Currently, Los Angeles, Miami, and New York are the major gateway cities for the influx of MDMA from abroad.
- In 2000, U.S. law enforcement seized 7 labs. In 2001, the number of MDMA clandestine labs seized in the U.S. increased to 17.
- Domestically, the DEA seized more than 1 million MDMA tablets in 1999, 3.3 million in 2000, and more than 5.5 million in 2001. The amount of seizures made by Customs has increased from 400,000 in 1997 to 7.2 million in 2001.
- GHB, GHB kits, and recipes for making GHB can be found on the Internet. In 2001, the DEA, along with State and local law enforcement seized 13 labs used to produce GHB. This is down from 20 GHB labs seized in 2000.

- Rohypnol, legally produced and sold in Latin America and Europe, is typical smuggled into the U.S. using mail or delivery services. States along the U.S. border with Mexico have most significant activity related to Rohypnol being mailed or brought into the U.S. via couriers from Mexico.
- Since the mid-1990's the number of Rohypnol seized in the U.S. have decreased. In 1995, a high of 164,534 dosage units of Rohypnol were seized, while in 2000, less than 5,000 dosage units were seized.
- DEA has reported an increase of seizures of ketamine from 4,551 dosage units in 1999, to 1,154,463 in 2000. In addition DEA data also indicates that 581,677 dosage units were seized from January to June of 2001.
- MDMA is a Schedule I drug as of 1998.
- GHB is a Schedule I drug as of 2000.
- Rohypnol is a Schedule IV drug as of 1984.
- Ketamine is a Schedule III drug as of 1999.
- We will look at the laws and scheduling of drugs in another chapter.

Street Terms for GHB	Street Terms for Ketamine
Goop	Cat Valium
Grievous bodily harm	K
Max	Jet
Soap	Super Acid

Street Terms for MDMA	Street Term for Rohypnol
Disco Biscuit	Forget Me Drug
Hug Drug	Mexican Valium
Go	Roaches
XTC	Roofies

Chapter Three
Understanding Controlled Substances

Controlled Substances

Understanding controlled substances: Not all drugs are narcotics; drugs are broken down into categories and schedules. The categories are narcotics, depressants, stimulants, hallucinogens, and cannabis. The schedules are I, II, III, IV, and V. Each category has a schedule number. Information about that particular drug such as trade or other names, medical use, physical dependence, psychological dependence, tolerance, duration of effects in hours, usual method of administration, possible effects, effects of overdose, and withdraw syndrome is documented.

Criminal Penalties for Trafficking (First Offense)
Schedule I Narcotic 15 years / $25,000 fine; Non-Narcotic 5 years / $15,000 fine
Schedule II Narcotic 15 years / $25,000 fine; Non Narcotic 5 years / $15,000 fine
Schedule III Narcotic 5 years / $15,000 fine; Non Narcotic 5 years / $15,000 fine
Schedule IV Narcotic 3 years / $10,000 fine; Non Narcotic 3 years / $10,000 fine
Schedule V Narcotic 1 year / $5,000 fine; Non Narcotic 1 year / $5,000 fine.

NARCOTICS
The following are classified as narcotics in the
State of Maryland:
Opium schedule II, III, and V
Morphine schedule II, III
Codeine schedule II, III, and V
Heroin schedule I
Hydromorphone schedule II

Meperidine (Pethidine) schedule II
Methadone schedule II

Withdraw From Narcotics
Watery eyes, runny nose, loss of appetite, irritability,
tremors, panic, chills, sweating, cramps, and nausea

Effects of Overdosing From Narcotics
Slow and shallow breathing, clammy skin,
convulsions, coma, and possible death

Possible Effects From Narcotics
Euphoria, drowsiness, respiratory depression,
constricted pupils, and nausea

How Long the Effects of Narcotics Will Last
Methadone 12-24 hours, other narcotics 3-6 hours

Method of Using Narcotics
Oral, smoked, injected, or sniffed

Physical and Psychological Dependence
High with exception of Codeine and that is moderate

DPRESSANTS
The following are classified as depressants in the
State of Maryland:
Chioral Hydrate schedule IV
Barbiturates schedule II, III, and IV
Glutethimide schedule III
Mathaqualone schedule II
Benzodiazepines IV

Withdrawal From Depressants
Anxiety, insomnia, tremors, delirium, convulsions,
and possible death

Effects From Overdosing From Depressants

Shallow respiration, cold and clammy skin, dilated pupils, weak and rapid pulse, coma, and possible death

Possible Effects From Depressants

Slurred speech, disorientation drunken behavior without odor of alcohol

How Long The Effects of Depressants Will Last

Chioral Hydrate 5-8 hours
Barbiturates 1-16 hours
All others 4-8 hours

Method of Using Depressants

Oral or injected

Physical and Psychological Dependence

Barbiturates high to moderate
Gluethimide and Methaqualone high
Benzodiazepines low

STIMULANTS

The following drugs are classified as stimulants in the State of Maryland:
Cocaine schedule II
Amphetamines schedule II and III
Phenmetrazine and Methylphenidate schedule II

Withdraw From Stimulants

Apathy, long periods of sleep, irritability, depression, and disorientation

Effects From Overdosing From Stimulants

Agitation, increase in body temperature, hallucinations, convulsions, and possible death

Possible Effects From Stimulants
Increased alertness, excitation,
euphoria, increased pulse rate and blood pressure,
insomnia, and loss of appetite

How long Will The Effects Stimulants Last
2-4 hours

Method of Using Stimulants
Oral or injected

Physical and Psychological Dependence
Physical dependence is possible
Psychological dependence is high

HALLUCINOGENS
The following drugs are classified a hallucinogens in
the State of Maryland:
LSD schedule I
Mescaline and Peyote schedule I
Amphetamine Variants schedule I
Phencyclidine schedule II
Phencyclidine Analogs schedule I

Withdraw From Hallucinogens
Withdraw syndrome is not reported

Effects From Overdosing From Hallucinogens
Longer more intense "trip" episodes, psychosis,
and possible death

Possible Effects From Hallucinogens
Illusions and hallucinations,
poor perception of time and distance

How Long Will The Effects of Hallucinogens Last
LSD 8-12 hours
Mescaline, Peyote, and Amphetamine Variants
Phencyclidine, Phencyclidine Analogs
Variable with these drugs

Method of Using Hallucinogens
LSD is taken orally
Mescaline, Peyote, and Amphetamine Variants
are injected or taken orally
Phencyclidine and Phencyclidine Analogs
are smoked, taken orally, or injected

Physical and Psychological Dependence
LSD, Mescaline, and Peyote have no physical dependency
Amphetamine Variants is unknown for it's physical dependency.
Phencyclidine and Phencyclidine Analogs have an unknown
degree of physical dependency.
LSD, Mescaline, Peyote, and Amphetamine Variants
have an unknown degree of psychological dependency.
Phencyclidine has a high degree of psychological dependency.
Phencyclidine Analogs have an unknown degree of
psychological dependency.

CANNABIS
The following drugs are classified as cannabis in the
State of Maryland:
Marijuana schedule I
Tetrahydrocannabinol schedule I
Hashish schedule I
Hashish Oil schedule I

Withdraw From Cannabis
Insomnia, hyperactivity, and decreased appetite occasionally
reported

Effects From Overdosing With Cannabis
Fatigue, paranoia, possible psychosis

Possible Effects From Cannabis
Euphoria, relaxed inhibitions, increased appetite,
disoriented behavior

How Long Will The Effects if Cannabis Last
2-4 hours

Method of Using Cannabis
Smoked or taken orally

Physical and Psychological Dependency
Degree of physical dependency is unknown
Degree of psychological dependency is moderate

- The legal foundation for the federal strategy of reducing the consumption of illicit drugs is the Comprehensive Drug Abuse Prevention and Control Act of 1970, Title II of which is more familiarly known as the Controlled Substance Act. (Public Law 91-513)
- The Drug Enforcement Administration better known as the DEA enforces the Controlled Substances Act.
- There are nine major control mechanisms imposed on the manufacturing, purchasing, and distributing of substances listed under the Act: (1) registration of handlers; (2) record keeping requirements; (3) quotas on manufacturing; (4) restrictions on distribution; (5) restrictions on dispensing; (6) limitations on imports and exports; (7) conditions for storage of drugs; (8) reports on transactions to the government and (9) criminal, civil, and administrative penalties for illegal acts. Some controls are equally applicable to substances listed in every schedule; the others vary, depending upon the schedule involved.

Registration: Any person who handles or intends to handle controlled substances must obtain a registration issued by DEA. A unique number is assigned to each legitimate handler of controlled drugs: importer, exporter, manufacturer, wholesaler, hospital, pharmacy, physician, and researcher. The customer prior to the purchase of a controlled substances must make this number available to the supplier.

Record keeping: The control mechanism applicable to all substances under control, regardless of the schedule in which they are placed, is a requirement that full records be kept of all quantities manufactured, purchases, sales, and inventories of the substances by each handler. There are limited exemptions from this requirement available to physicians and researchers.

There is one distinction between schedule items for record keeping requirements. Records for Schedule I and II drugs must be kept separate from all other records of the handler; records for Schedule III, IV, and V substances must be kept in a "ready retrievable" form.

Quotas: DEA limits the quantity of controlled substances listed in Schedule I and II which can be produced during any given calendar year. Using available data on sales and inventories of controlled substances in Schedules I and II, and taking into account substances of drug abuse, DEA establishes aggregate production quotas, which set the national limits of production.

Distributions: The keeping of records is required for distributions of a controlled substance from one manufacturer to another, from manufacturer to wholesaler, from importer to wholesaler, and from wholesaler to dispenser. In the case of Schedule I and II drugs, the supplier must have a special order form (222) from the DEA. This form is issued by the DEA for persons who are properly registered in Schedule I and II. For drugs in Schedules III, IV, and V, no order form is necessary. The supplier in each case, however, is under an obligation to verify the authenticity of his customer. The supplier is held fully accountable for any drugs which are shipped to a purchaser who does not have a valid registration.

Dispensing to Patients: The dispensing of a controlled substance is the delivery of the controlled substance to the ultimate user, who may be a patient or research subject.

Schedule I drugs are those which have no currently accepted medical use in the United States; they may therefore be used only in research situations. For schedule II, III, and IV medications, a prescription order is required under the Federal Food, and Drug and Cosmetic Act. Schedule II prescription order must be written and signed by the practitioner; they may not be telephoned into the pharmacy except in an emergency. In addition, the prescription may not be refilled; the patient must see the physician again in order to obtain more drugs.

Import and Export: Any international transactions involving any drug in Schedule I or II, or a narcotic in Schedule III must have prior approval of the DEA. International transactions involving a non-narcotic in Schedule III or any drug in Schedule IV or V must be made with prior notice to the DEA without requiring its approval.

Security for Storage of Drugs: DEA sets the requirement for the security of premises, which contain controlled substances as a condition to registration under Section 303 of the Act. In the case of Schedule I and II drugs, exceptionally high security requirements are imposed: a specially constructed vault with reinforced concrete walls and a steel gate, a 24 hour alarm system, and immediate availability of security guards, are required. For drugs in Schedule III, IV and V, the vault is an optional feature. These costly special requirements for storage apply only to manufacturers, importers, exporters, and wholesalers of controlled drugs. They do not apply to qualifying researchers, physicians, pharmacies, and hospitals; in these cases reduced security requirements are imposed to correlate drugs.

Reports to DEA: Periodic reports regarding transactions in certain drugs must be submitted to DEA. The Automation of Reports and Consolidated Orders System (ARCOS), established in January 1974, carry out the monitoring of all drugs in Schedule I and II and narcotic drugs in Schedule III. Manufactures, wholesalers, importers, and exporters of any of these drugs must report all manufacturing activities, all importations and exportations, and all other distributions to the DEA; inventories must also be filed annually.

Criminal Penalties for Trafficking: We have already viewed the penalties for trafficking for first offenders; the following are the penalties for trafficking drugs for the second offended.

Schedule I, Narcotic: Max. Imprison 30 yrs, Max. Fine 50K, Min., Parole 6 yrs.

Schedule 1, Non – Narcotic: Max. Imprison 10 yrs, Max Fine 30K Min. Parole 4 yrs.

Schedule I, Narcotic: Max. Imprison 30 yrs, Max. Fine 50k, Min Parole 6 yrs.

Schedule II, Non – Narcotic: Max Imprison 10 yrs, Max Fine 30K, Min Parole 4 yrs.

Schedule III, Narcotic: Max Imprison 10 yrs, Max Fine 30K, Min Parole 4 yrs.

Schedule III, Non-Narcotic: Max Imprison 10 yrs, Max Fine 30K, Min. Parole 4 yrs.

Schedule IV, Narcotic: Max Imprison 6 yrs, Max. Fine 20K, Min Parole 2 yrs.

Schedule IV, Non-Narcotic: Max Imprison 6 yrs, Max. Fine 20K, Min. Parole 2 yrs.

Schedule V, Narcotic: Max Imprison 2 yrs, Max Fine 10K, Min. Parole 0 yrs.

Schedule V, Non – Narcotic: Max Imprison 2 yrs, Max Fine 10K, Min. Parole 0 yrs.

Criteria by which drugs are scheduled: The Controlled Substances Act sets forth the findings which must be made to put a substance in any of the five schedules. These are as follows: (section 202b).

Schedule I
   A. The drug or other substance has a high potential for abuse.
   B. The drug or other substances has no currently accepted medical use in treatment in the United States.

C. There is a lack of accepted safety for use of the drug or other substance under medical supervision.

Schedule II

A. The drug or other substances has a high potential for abuse.

B. The drug or other substance has a currently accepted medical use in treatment in the United States or currently accepted medical use with severe restrictions.

C. Abuse of the drug or other substances may lead to severe psychological or physical dependence.

Schedule III

A. The drug or other substance has a potential for abuse less than the drug or other substances in Schedules I and II.

B. The drug or other substances has a currently accepted medical use in treatment in the United States.

C. Abuse of the drug or other substances may lead to moderate to low physical dependence or high psychological dependence.

Schedule IV

A. The drug or other substances has a low potential for abuse relative to the drugs or other substances in Schedule II.

B. The drug or other substance has a currently accepted medical use in treatment in the United States.

C. Abuse of the drug or other substances may lead to limited physical dependence or psychological dependence relative to the drugs or other substances in Schedule III.

Schedule V

A. The drug or other substance has a low potential for abuse relative to the drugs or other substances in Schedule IV.

B. The drug or other substances has a currently accepted medical use in treatment in the United States.

C. Abuse of the drug or other substance may lead to limited physical dependence or psychological dependence relative to the drugs or other substances in Schedule IV.

Chapter Four
The Addict's Story
A Parent's Advice

MISS HEROIN

So now little man, you've grown tired of grass,
L.S.D., goofballs, cocaine, and hash;
And someone, pretending to be a true friend,
Said. "I'll introduce you to Miss Heroin".
Well, honey, before you start fooling with me,
Just let me inform you on how it will be.
For, I will seduce you and make you my slave.
I've sent men much stronger than you to their graves.

You think you could never become a disgrace
And end up addicted to poppy seed waste.
So, you'll start inhaling me one afternoon,
You'll then take me into your arms very soon.
And once I have entered deep down in your veins,
The carving will nearly drive you insane.

You'll need lots of money (as you have been told)
For darling, I'm more expensive than gold.
You'll swindle your mother; and, just for a buck
You'll turn into something vile and corrupt.
You'll mug and you'll steal for my narcotic charm,
And feel contentment when I'm in your arms.

The day you realize the monster you've grown,
You'll solemnly promise to leave me alone.
If you think that you've got the mystical knack,
Then sweetie, just try getting me off your back.

The vomit the cramps, your gut tied in a knot,
The jangling nerves screaming for just one more shot.
The cold chills and hot sweat, and withdraw pains,
Can only be saved by my little white grains
There's no other way, and there's no need to look,
For deep down inside, you will know you are hooked.

You'll desperately run to the pusher and then,
You'll welcome me back to your arms once again.
And when you return, just as I for told!
I know that you'll give me your body and soul

You've given your morals, your conscience, you're heart
and you will be mine until **DEATH DO US PART**.

By Anonymous

An Addict's Story

In addiction everyone's story is different. Some involve themselves in prostitution, theft, and con games; others become homeless and walk the streets hungry. Some are unaware they are infected with HIV or that they are even dieing with Aids, while others become masters of manipulation. It is even possible for an addict to commit murder. However, one thing that every addict has in common is the disease of addiction. Whether you are addicted to heroin, cocaine, alcohol, pharmaceuticals drugs, or your drug of choice, addiction can cause you and your family pain and suffering.

I was asked what it was like to be addicted. For me it was like being trapped under ice, being able to see the surface, but not being able to reach it. Being addicted is like every principle, every moral that was instilled in me was never there. Everyday of my life I could feel another piece of my soul leaving my body, every breath you take gets shorter and every day gets longer. To anyone who has never felt this, be very thankful, for anyone who has felt this, I feel for you. If you are still feeling this, there are alternative endings.

My name is Josh, I am 28 years old and I took my first drink when I was 12 years old. At age 13 I tried marijuana. I used both of them recreationally. When I was 18, I met my love and my worst enemy, heroin. After using heroin for a year and a half, I wanted to stop. I was tired and everyday was the same; the sickness, runny nose, backaches, my leg ached, my stomach was in knots, and I had diarrhea. The only way to stop the sickness was by doing more heroin.

After 3 1/2 years, I was using 7 to 8 pills a day. At night, I found myself in places that most people would not go in broad daylight. I remember it was after midnight, I met these people and wanted to buy from them. I was forced to snort some dope at gunpoint, just to prove I wasn't a cop. I was getting tired of being tired so I asked for help and went to an outpatient program. I had to go there everyday for a week just to get enough medicine to make me feel better.

I had not used heroin for years, I moved from Baltimore to Knoxville, Tennessee. There I found new friends who owned a tattoo shop. Even though I stopped using heroin, I was still drinking and smoking pot. Before I knew it, I started eating pills and drinking even more alcohol. I used cocaine to stay awake, and then I started having blackouts. I woke up one morning in jail and didn't know how I got there. One day I woke up in my apartment with the door kicked in, I was lying on the floor in a pile of splinters wondering what happened. I also remember the day I woke up sleeping next to a dumpster, wondering how I got there. I told myself, "that's what happens when you party hard".

It wasn't long and I found myself back in Baltimore hoping to leave my problems behind. However, my addiction followed me. I went to a bar about 2:00 in the afternoon; I started drinking and eating pills. The next thing I remembered, I was in the hospital in the intensive care unit with a bruised frontal lobe and bleeding in the back of my brain. After 2 weeks in the hospital, I was released but was bed ridden for another month. I went back to Knoxville hoping again to leave my problems behind. But I soon realized that I could not run from my addiction. No matter where I went, my old friends, alcohol and drugs came with me.

When I used I was like another person, when I tried to stop I was like another person. I was being pulled apart by the drugs and alcohol and noone could save me.

During my addiction, I was known to throw Christmas gifts in the yard and kick the paper off the boxes. I threw a glass of water on my brothers computer. I was mad at the world and the lifestyle I was living. To put it mildly, I was not a nice person.

I slacked off the alcohol only after I was introduced to Oxycontin. Oxycontin is a pharmaceutical grade of heroin. I used

Oxy's for about four years; when I finally stopped, I was taking 2 to 4 80 milligrams a day and eating xanex to go to sleep.

The feeling of eating Oxycontin gives you is the same feeling that heroin gives you. During this period of using, I isolated myself from family and friends. After getting in trouble at work several times and my family repeatedly telling me I need help I went to the Hudson House in Salisbury, Maryland. I was there for a 22-day treatment program; 17 of those days were for detox. What I did not know was that taking the xanax that I used for sleeping could have caused seizures when coming off of it. So I was given medication to control these seizures. After being released from the Hudson House, I had no plans to ever use drugs again, no heroin, no Oxycontin, not even pot, I was finished or at least I thought I was.

I did drink from time to time but I thought I could stop whenever I wanted to. But all drinking was doing was fueling my addiction. One day at work I started getting pains in my leg. The pain was like something I had never felt before. I went to the hospital and got an x-ray. I was told that I had a bone tumor and was given pain medicine. Everyone told me that it was not a good idea to take the pain pills but I thought I could handle it. Guess what? It wasn't long before I was back with old friends and going to old places. I had four doctors giving me prescriptions. I soon had to endure an operation on my leg to remove the tumor. The medicine kept coming and I was out of work for over seven months. By this time my, addiction was going strong. Then the medicine stopped suddenly. Then an old friend stopped by with some heroin and we snorted. Then next day, I wanted more and before long I was up to 16 pills a day. I was worse than I have ever been in my life. One pill cost $10.00, but I convinced myself that if I used intravenously my habit would be cheaper. Within 4 weeks of that first shot, I sold everything I owned. I sold from my father; I was held-up at gunpoint and sold personal things that belonged to my friends. I loaned my car to someone to get dope, he was in a hit and run accident with my car. I took gas from garages to put in my car. I was so bad that my grandmother was afraid of me. I was writing one bad check after another.

In just 7 weeks, I obtained a habit that I could no longer keep up with. I ate a box of macaroni and cheese, or Romen noodles everyday just to have some food in my stomach. I walked around with no shoelaces sometimes because I would use them to tie off my arm to shoot up the heroin. When I made it to work, my lunch box did not contain a regular lunch; it contained a needle, some water, a spoon, a lighter, and of course some heroin. That was my life, and I lived it everyday.

My mom, brother, and dad never gave up on me. My dad called my workplace and got me fired from a $20.00 an hour job. He then called the school I was attending for Local 24 and told them about my problem. It wasn't long before everything was gone.

My job, my car, my home, everything I owned, I was at the end of my rope. I then asked my brother to take me back to the Hudson House for inpatient rehab.

It was after this stay that I realized that I could not possess the ability to use drugs or alcohol. Not even socially. I came to realize I could not use any substance that would change the way I feel. Believing this was the foundation for my recovery. I moved into a half-way house, which I was very apprehensive about. However, that move was one of the best things I ever did. I became actively involved in a twelve-step program. These programs are not to stop you from using; they are programs to show you how to start living life without drugs.

When I was using, I had no structure in my life; I never took responsibility seriously. Now I see life through a different set of eyes. I am actually learning how to live life on life's terms. My mother said, "Josh I have put you in God's hands". Today, I thank God for watching over me.

I never gave much thought of how much pain I caused my mom, dad, and brother. But I do realize they were watching me kill myself. I thought because I never abused them that I wasn't hurting them. Mental pain is a pain that keeps on hurting. If you can't see the pain on someone's face it doesn't mean it's not there. The repercussions of my past still haunt me, some of the people I have known won't even talk to me because of the things

I have done to them. And apologizing is not enough. If I could go back and live my life over again things would be different. Today I have such an appreciation for life, for people who care and for my family.

How I lived through it all is truly amazing. But I am glad I am here to share this story with you. These are only a few things that I have experienced, but I hope that someone will read this and think twice before they decide to get married to heroin. The biggest mistake that you make is believing that you can control the drug, when in fact the drug controls you.

There are a few things I would like to say to parents, watch your child's actions. Isolation is one of the things I did when I didn't want my family to know what I was doing. Some signs are not as clear as others. Maybe a bottle of eye drops in a book bag to cover the red eyes from smoking weed, or the drastic change in moods, will help you detect drug use in your child. When I was using I would be very temperamental, my mood would change at the drop of a hat. When I used heroin or others opiates, I had dilated pupils (black part of the eye gets very tiny looking like a point of a pencil). I became very defensive when my parents asked me about my drug use. I would argue with them until I was blue in the face, trying all along to convince them I was not high. On sunny days I would make an excuse to stay outside in the sunlight, using the sun as an excuse for the dilated pupils.

So what is the best defense against drugs and your child? Education and questions. Learn about the drugs your child is using and keep asking questions. Remember, the more you know, the better chances you have in dealing with this problem.

By
Josh Wright

A Parent's Advice

I see the tears and hear the pathetic stories of addicted people all day long. Parents and family members ask me for advice then go right back enabling their loved one in their addictions, thinking things will be better in the morning. Well things don't get betting in the morning, you MUST do something NOW if your loved one is going to survive the streets and get off drugs.

I am a retired undercover narcotics officer. I never thought my son would ever become addicted to heroin, but he did. I lived in the hellish nightmare of finding him dead in his bed from an overdose of heroin for years. And even though he is clean today, I still worry about him and he is twenty-eight years old. I still check out his stories and seek the truth about where he has been or where he is going. My son almost died because of his addiction, but I was determined that I was not going to lose him to the streets.

My wife and I are both college graduates BUT that did not keep our son from becoming an addict. We lived in a good neighborhood, BUT that did not stop our son from becoming an addict. We owned our own home and had a good income, BUT that did not stop our son from becoming an addict. We did our best as parents to encourage our son to make right choices in life, BUT that did not stop our son from becoming an addict. So where did our son learn this behavior? His drug use was a choice like every thing we do in life is a choice. As parents we chose to love Josh even with his heroin addiction; we knew that love and understanding would play a big part in his recovery. However, Josh's mom was more the praying type than I was. I wanted to get to the source of his problem.

I came out of retirement and I did what I had to do in order for my son to live another day. My approach was more police like

93

than father like. You may not agree with what I did, but I thought, "I can't talk to a tombstone". I did what I thought was best, call it luck or answered prayer, my son is alive today and I don't regret one thing that I did to stop the drug use.

Here are the steps to take if your child is on drugs. I hope you can be encouraged and that you will find the strength to face the truth; what is the truth? The truth is if you don't stop it now tomorrow may be too late.

- Stop making excuses and except the fact your child is an addict.
- When you say NO! mean NO!
- Check the mileage on the car before and after use. Question as to where your child has gone.
- Get a voice activated reorder and put it in their room or hook it to their telephone.
- Question their friends when you suspect something is going on.
- Write down phone numbers and tag numbers, keep a log with all information in it. If needed to turn it over to the police.
- Check your pills and count them everyday.
- Follow your child if necessary.
- Search their room (read the chapter on hiding drugs)
- If you find drugs call the police and have them arrested. DO NOT get them out of jail or call an attorney. If you do you're spending more money and saying to them "your not guilty of this crime".
- Confront them with questions and stay focused.
- Ask them to take a drug test; but make sure you are in the room when they take it. Do not let them tell you when they are going to take the test because they will use someone else's urine if they can get away with it.
- Make them do the calling for all appointments, you're not their secretary.
- Stop calling them for work if they lose the job chances are they have been using the money to buy drugs with anyway.

94

- Do not make excuses for them with the family.
- Stop paying their bills and never sign a loan to help them out of their situation.
- Never give cash to them if you suspect a drug problem.
- Always remember anger is control and communication is fact.
- Never give in to their arguments, an addict knows just how to manipulate you.
- Give deadlines and stick to it, even if they become homeless.
- Always make them earn back your trust and remember addiction is not cured over night.
- If you suspect they are going out after you go to bed, put a penny on one of the tires, if the penny is on the ground the next morning then you know the car has been moved.
- Check the gas in your car and the garage, an addict is know to steal gas for their own automobile and most of the time this is where it comes from.
- Never leave money laying around.
- If you think they will steal from you set them up, put $20.00 out and leave the room. If it is gone when you come back in the room, confront them. Let them know you set them up.
- Take all keys away and tell them if they are late coming in they sleep outside.
- If they lose there transportation, tell them to get a bus pass.
- Take pictures of their friends and their cars, and tell them your giving information to the police. (do this only if you suspect drug use)
- Confront every situation and never leave thinking, "I should have ask them where they were going". Or "What they were doing".
- If you smell incenses in the room look around for the pot. Do a surprise raid and let them know who's house their in.
- If they get mad, believe me they will get over it.
- You MUST do every thing you can to save your child's life.

Here are some things I did to save my son's life

- I searched his house when he was there and when he wasn't there. If he said he was calling the police and have me arrested I would have said, "And when I get out of jail I still come back and we will do this drill again until you understand it's going to stop". I was relentless in my quest to save his life.
- I set him up with pain pills to see if he would take them, he did. And I called the police and made a report. I had one year to have him arrested. I use that as a tool to get him into treatment.
- I went up and down the street where he lived and told people he was working with me and he was going to arrest them if they sold him drugs. My son told me I was going to get him killed. I said, "your going to die anyway."
- I had police stop him in his car just to let him know I was watching.
- I had the police helicopter shine a light on his house.
- I called his boss and got him fired from a $20.00 an hour job. He was using the money for drugs anyway.
- I called his union and told them he was addicted and could hurt a co-worker.
- I called his local and advised his teachers that he had a problem, he was removed from class and lost out in his third year apprentice program.
- I called the doctor and told him I was coming after him if he gave my son another prescription.
- I threw everyone out of my son's house including my son, because the house belonged to me.
- I went to where he pawned personal things and advised them that most of the things were personal things from other people.
- I took my son to the funeral home when someone lost a son or daughter so he could see the pain that families went through because of drug addiction.

- I followed my son and had others follow him and reported all activity to the local authorities.
- I made promises to people that if my son died because of his addiction that I would be hunting the dealer or dealers that sold to him, I had no fear of their retaliation.
- I talked to my son's friend's parents and told them to call the police on him if they had anything missing and thought that he took it.
- I let my son lose every thing he had from his home, his car, his insurance, and his personal property. It all had to go. I was only concerned about one thing, keeping him alive.
- My son knows I did all of this because I loved him. I guess if I had of lost him to the streets that I knew in my heart that I did all I could to save him. But I also knew that he was making the choices in life. I would give my life to save my children from a life of drug addiction.

Chapter Five
Maryland Law

Nationwide

We are the most violent nation in the world. Crime has become part of our everyday life; we have made excuses for the criminals and opened the doors to jails and prisons and set them free. The public cry is, "protect our children and make our streets safe", while the fact remains the courts are letting criminals go with a slap on the wrist.

So just how safe are we in America? At the moment we are concentrating on terrorism; however, after you read this report, YOU will make sure your doors are locked. The real terrorists are the drug dealers and gangs that roam our streets like packs of wolves that hunt their victims in the wild.

Looking at crime statistics nationwide in 1980, we reported 1,344,520 violent crimes, 12,063,700 crimes against property, 23,040 murders, 82,990 rapes, 565,840 robberies, 672,650 aggravated assaults, 3,327,700 burglaries, and 7,136,900 larcenies.

In 1990, just ten years later, we reported 1,820,013 violent crimes, 12,131,900 crimes against property, 23,440 murders, 102,560 rapes, 639,270 robberies, 1,054,860 aggravated assaults, 3,073,900 burglaries, and 7,945,700 larcenies.

In 2000, we reported 1,424,289 violent crimes, 10,181,462 crimes against property, 15,517 murders, 407,842 robberies, 90,9186 rapes, 910,744 aggravated assaults, 2,049,946 burglaries, and 6,965,957 larcenies. The source of this information came from http://www.disastercenter.com/crime/uscrime.thm

Maryland
Taken from The "Digest of Criminal Laws"

Let's look at a few vocabulary words. These words will be important in understanding Maryland law.

Attempt: The punishment of a person who is convicted of an attempt to commit a crime may not exceed the maximum punishment for the crime attempted. Criminal Law Article 1-201

Conspiracy: A plan or understanding between 2 or more persons to commit an unlawful act. The crime is completed when the agreement is entered into. The punishment cannot exceed the maximum punishment allowable for the crime that was conspired to commit. Criminal Law Article 1-202

Accessory: (Before the fact) An accessory before the fact may be charged, tried, convicted and sentenced for a crime regardless of whether the principle in the crime has been convicted or even charged with that crime. Criminal Procedure Article 4:204. (After the fact) To be charged as an accessory after the fact, the accessory must take some action to assist the felon, avoid the consequences of his crime, and must not be guilty of the underlying felony as a principle. Note: Maryland law does not seem to authorize charging accessory after the fact to a misdemeanor, and instead takes the approach that all involved in misdemeanor are chargeable as principals. Unless otherwise provided by law, a person who is convicted of being an accessory after the fact to a felony is guilty of a felony and on conviction is subject to the lesser of:

- Imprisonment not to exceed 5 years.
- A penalty not to exceed the maximum penalty provided by law for committing the underlying felony. Criminal law Article 1-301.

Arrest: It is generally recognized that an arrest is the taking, seizing, or detaining of a person by another.

- By touching or putting hands on him.
- By any act that indicates an intention to take him into custody and that subjects him to actual control and will of the person making the arrest.
- By the consent of the person to be arrested. Bouldin v State, 276 Md. 511, 515-516 (1976)

There are four elements that constitute a legal arrest.

- An intent to arrest
- Under a real or pretended authority
- Accompanied by a seizure or detention of the person
- Which is understood by the person arrested

Correctional Officers, Parole, and Probation Officers: Correctional employees monitoring inmates on home detention and parole and probation officers supervising offenders on home detention have the same powers to arrest these individuals as are set forth in this title for police officers. Correctional officers in local correctional facilities designated by the managing official under Sec.11-802 of the Correctional Services Article, have the same powers to arrest persons on the property of the facility as are set forth in this title for police officers. Criminal Procedure Article Sec. 2-207

Vehicle Law Arrest: A police officer may arrest, without a warrant, a person for a violation of the Maryland Vehicle Law including any rule or regulation adopted under it, or for a violation of any traffic law or ordinance of any local authority of this State, "IF":

- If the person has committed or is committing the violation within the view or presence of the officer, and the violation is any of the following.
- A violation of 22-111 or 24-111.1 of this Article, relating to the failure or refusal to submit a vehicle to a weighing or to remove excess weight from it.
- The officer has reasonable grounds to believe that a person will disregard a traffic citation.

- The person has committed or is committing the violation within the view or presence of the officer, and either the person does not furnish satisfactory evidence of identity or; that the officer has reasonable grounds to believe that the person will disregard a traffic citation.
- The officer has probable cause to believe that the person has committed the violation, and the violation is any of the following offenses; driving or attempting to drive while intoxicated or while under the influence of alcohol; driving or attempting to drive while under the influence of any drug, any combination of drugs and alcohol or while under the influence of any controlled dangerous substance; failure to stop, give information, or render reasonable assistance, as required by subsection 20-102 and 20-104 of this Article, in the event of an accident resulting in bodily injury to or death of any person; driving or attempting to drive a motor vehicle while the driver's licenses or privilege to drive is suspended or revoked; failure to stop or give information, as to required by subsection 20-103 through 20-105 of this Article, in the event of an accident resulting in damage to a vehicle or other property; any offense that causes or contributed to an accident resulting in bodily injury or death of any person; fleeing or attempting to elude a Police Officer; the person is a non resident and the officer has probable cause to believe that person has committed the violation and the violation contributed to the accident; the officer has probable cause to believe that the person has committed the violation and, subject to the procedures set forth in section 26-203 of this subtitle, the person is issued a traffic citation and refuses to acknowledge its receipt by signature.
- An arrest under this section shall be made in the same manner as, and without more force than, in misdemeanor cases.
- A person arrested under this section shall be taken without unnecessary delay before the District Court

Commissioner, as specified in section 26-401 of this title, unless the arresting officer in his discretion releases the individual upon the individual's written promise to appear for trial Transportation Article 26-202.

Assistance In Making Arrest: If an officer orders a driver to assist him in enforcing the law or making an arrest, the officer's employer (government unit) is liable for the damages caused by the officer's negligence. Transportation Article 19-101. Officers may not direct any driver, owner, or passenger of a vehicle to participate in a roadblock. If this happens, the officer's employer (government unit) is liable for resulting damages, regardless of whether the officer was negligent. Transportation Article 19-102.

- The old common law made it a crime for citizens to refuse to assist a police officer. Over the years, that rule changed to disallow commandeering citizen's cars for roadblocks, and to provide for compensation for officer's negligence. Maryland case law does not rule out the possibility of police authority to summons citizens to assist in enforcing the law; but does not provide what the limits of authority may be. Keesling v. State, 288 Md. 579, 585-589 and note 2 (1980).

Force In Making An Arrest: Any force used must be reasonable under the circumstances, exactly what is "reasonable" is not capable of precise definition, but depends on the facts and circumstances of each particular case, as judged by the perspective of a reasonable officer on the scene. Graham v. Connor, 409 U.S. 386, 109 S. Ct. 1865 (1989). Generally, officers should use the least amount of force that is necessary to control an incident, effect an arrest, or take the prisoner into custody. If however, he is resisting he may repel force with force. A prudent officer, in making an arrest, should always consider the enormity of the crime and character of resistance, and use only such force as may be necessary to overcome the resistance and make the arrest.

Warrant Less Entry: The 4th Amendment to the Constitution requires that police entering into a dwelling must knock on the door and announce their identity and purpose before attempting forcible entry. The knock and the announce requirement may give way if circumstances present a threat of physical violence, or if police have reason to believe evidence would be destroyed if advance notice is given. Wilson v. Arkansas, 514 U.S. 927, 115 S. Ct. 1914 (1995)

To justify a no knock entry, police must have reasonable suspicion that knocking and announcing their presence, under the particular circumstances, would be dangerous or futile, or it would inhibit the effective investigation of the crime by, for example, allowing destruction of evidence. Richards v. Wisconsin, 520 U.S. 385, 117 S Ct. 1416 (1997)

There is no automatic exception to the knock-and-announce requirements for felony drug investigation.

Exigent circumstances may justify a warrantless entry. Maryland courts consider the following in deciding if exigent circumstances exist:

- That a grave offense is involved.
- That the suspect is reasonably believed to be armed.
- That there exists more than minimum probable cause based upon reasonably trustworthy information to believe that the suspect committed the crime involved.
- That there is strong reason to believe that the suspect is in the premises being entered.
- That there is a likelihood that the suspect will escape if not swiftly apprehended.
- That reasonableness of police attitude and conduct is demonstrated through circumstances demonstrating a peaceable entry. Gaynor v. State, 50 Md.App. 600, 603-604 (1982)

Entry With a Warrant: Generally, a police officer executing a search warrant must give proper notice of his purpose and authority and be denied admittance before he can use force to break and enter the premises to be searched. Exceptions to this general rule may apply if officers have announced their presence, exigent circumstances exist, or the warrant specifically authorizes a no-knock entry. Sate v. Lee, 374 Md. 275 (2003).

Fresh Pursuit: This section applies to law enforcement officers of a jurisdiction in the state who engages in fresh pursuit of a person in the state.

- Fresh pursuit is pursuit that is continuous and without unreasonable delay.
- Fresh pursuit need not be instant pursuit.
- In determining whether the pursuit meets the elements of fresh pursuit, a court shall apply the requirements of common law definition of fresh pursuit that relates to these elements.

A law enforcement officer may engage in fresh pursuit of a person who has:

- Has committed or is believed by law enforcement officers to have committed a felony in the jurisdiction in which the law enforcement has the power of arrest.
- Has committed a misdemeanor in the presence of the law enforcement officer in the jurisdiction in which the law enforcement officer has the power of arrest.

A law enforcement officer who is engaged in fresh pursuit of a person may:

- Arrest the person anywhere in the state and hold the person in custody and return the person to the jurisdiction in which a court has proper venue for the alleged to have been committed by the person. Criminal Procedure Article Sec. 2-301.

Search Warrants: Definition – a written order by a judicial officer commanding a peace officer to search and seize the property described. Md. Rule 4-10. Generally, a judge may issue a search warrant if there is probable cause to believe a crime is being committed on property, or there is property subjected to seizure on a person or a premises within the judges jurisdiction.

Requirements – The Maryland constitution prohibits general or vague warrants, and warrants that are not supported by a sworn statement (Md. Const, Decl. Of Rights, Art. 26). Specific warrants requirements are set forth in Criminal Procedure Article 1-203, and Md. Rule 4-601. Generally, search warrants must contain sufficient probable cause to justify searching and seizing and must be supported by a personal knowledge statement under oath (affidavit) describing the factual basis for probably cause.

The person and place to be searched must be described with particulars. The warrant must be served within 15 calendar days after it was issued, after which it expires and is void. The return must be made to the issuing judge, along with the inventory of property seized. Returned warrants are kept sealed, but may be viewed by persons whose property was seized or per court order.

Part of the information in the following came from the "Digest of Criminal Laws" and "Lexis Nexist". The reason I have combined them is to give you, the reader a better understanding of WHAT the penalty could be if you sell, possess or have in your control certain drugs. Chapter 3 gives you an understanding of controlled substances as to the Scheduling of drugs.

Drug Kingpin: "Drug Kingpin" defined – In this section, "drug kingpin" means an organizer, supervisor, financier, or manager who acts as a coconspirator in conspiracy to manufacture, distribute, dispense, transport in, or bring into the State, a control dangerous substance.

Drug kingpin conspiracy; penalty – A kingpin who conspires to manufacture, distribute, dispense, transport in, or bring into the State, a controlled, dangerous substance in amount listed in 5-612 of this subtitle (5-612 is found in volume dealer) is guilty of a felony. Conviction is subject to imprisonment for not less than 20 years and not to exceeding 40 years without the possibility of parole or a fine not to exceeding $1,000,000 or both.

- The court may not suspend any part of the mandatory minimum sentence of 20 years.
- A person is not eligible for parole during mandatory minimum sentence.
- Ultimate distributing or dispensing elsewhere not a defense; it is not a defense to a prosecution under this section that the controlled dangerous substance was brought into or transported in the state solely for ultimate distribution or dispensing in another jurisdiction.

- Merger, notwithstanding any other provision of this title, a conviction under this section does not merge with the conviction for any crime that is the object of the conspiracy.
- Probation before judgment; 6-220 of the Criminal procedure Article, does not apply to a conviction under this section.

Volume Dealer:

A. A person who violates 5-602 of this subtitle with respect to any of the following controlled dangerous substances in the amounts indicated, is subject on conviction, a fine not to exceed $100,00 and the enhanced penalty provided in subsection C of this section;

- 50 pounds or more of marijuana
- 448 grams or more of cocaine
- 448 grams or more of any mixture containing a detectable amount of cocaine.
- 50 grams or more of cocaine base, commonly know as "crack".
- 28 grams or more of morphine or opium or any derivative, salt, isomer, or salt of isomer of morphine or opium.
- Any mixture containing 28 grams or more of morphine or opium or any derivative, salt, isomer, or salt of an isomer of morphine or opium.
- 1,000 dosage units or more of lysergic acid diethyl amide (LSD).
- Any mixture containing the equivalent of 1,000 dosage units of lysergic acid diethyl amide (LSD).
- 16 ounces or more of phencyclidine (PCP) in liquid form.
- 448 grams or more of any mixture containing phencyclidine (PCP).
- 448 grams or more of methamphetamine or any mixture containing 448 grams or more of methamphetamine.

B. For the purpose of determining the quantity of a controlled dangerous substance involved in individual acts of manufacturing in subsection (A) of this section, the references of the "signature" of distributing, dispensing, or possessing with intent to manufacture, distribute, or dispense under subsection (A) of this section, the acts may be aggregated if each of the acts occurred within a 90-day period.

A person who is convicted under 5-602 of this subtitle with respect to a controlled dangerous substance in an amount indicated in subsection (A) of this section, shall be sentenced to imprisonment for not less that 5 years.

- The court may not suspend any part of the mandatory minimum sentences of five years.
- Except as provided in 4-305 of the Correctional Services Article, the person is not eligible for parole during the mandatory minimum sentences. Criminal Law Article 5-612.

Possessing or Administering Controlled dangerous Substance: Except as otherwise provided in this title, a person may not possess or administer to another, a controlled dangerous substance, unless obtained directly or by prescription from an authorized provider acting in the course of professional practice, or obtain or attempt to obtain a controlled dangerous substance, or procure or attempt to procure the administration of a controlled dangerous substance by;

(i)   fraud, deceit, misrepresentation, or subterfuge

(ii) the counterfeiting or alteration of a prescription or a written order

(iii) the concealment or a material fact

(iv) the use of a false name or address

(v)   falsely assuming the title of or representing to be a manufacturer, distributor, or authorized provider

(vi) making, issuing, or presenting a false or counterfeit prescription or written order.

Information not privileged – Information that is communicated to a physician in an effort to obtain a controlled dangerous substance in violation of this section is not a privileged communication.

Penalty; medical necessity,-

1.   Except as provided in paragraphs (2) and (3) of this subsection, a person who violates this section is guilty of a

misdemeanor and on conviction is subject to imprison-ment not exceeding 4 years or a fine not to exceed $25,000 or both.

2.   A person whose violation of this section involves the use or possession of marijuana is subject to imprisonment not exceeding 1 year or a fine not exceeding $1,000 or both.

3.   (i) In a prosecution for the use or possession of mari-juana, the defendant may introduce and the court shall consider as a mitigating factor any evidence of medical necessity.

(ii) Notwithstanding paragraph (2) of this subsection, if the court finds that the person used or possessed mari-juana because of medical necessity, on conviction of a violation of this section, the maximum penalty that the court may impose on the person is a fine not exceeding $100.

[An. Code 1957, art. 27, 287 (a), (e); 2002, ch. 26 2; 2003, ch. 21, 1 ch. 442]

Distributing Fake Controlled Dangerous Substances: A person may not distribute, attempt to distribute, or possess, with the intent to distribute a non-controlled substance:

•   that the person represents as a controlled dangerous substance
•   that the person intends for use or distribution as a con-trolled dangerous substance
•   under circumstances where one reasonably should know that the non-controlled substance will be used or distrib-uted for use as a controlled dangerous substance.

To determine if a person has violated this section, the court or other authority shall include in its consideration:

•   whether the non-controlled substances was packaged in a manner normally used to distribute a controlled danger-ous substance illegally
•   whether the distribution or attempted distribution included an exchange of, demand for money or other

property as consideration, and whether the amount of consideration was substantially greater than the reasonable value of the non-controlled substance

- whether the physical appearance of the non-controlled substance is substantially identical to that of a controlled dangerous substance.

A person who violates this section is guilty of a felony, and on conviction, is subject to imprisonment not exceeding 5 years or a fine not to exceed $15,000.

It is not a defense to a prosecution under this section that the defendant believes that the non-controlled substance was a controlled dangerous substance. Criminal Law Article 5-617.

Possession or Purchase of Non-controlled Substance: Except as authorized in this title, a person may not possess or purchase a non-controlled substance that the person reasonably believes is a controlled dangerous substances. To determine if a person has violated this section, the court shall include in its consideration;

- whether the non-controlled substances was packaged in a manner normally used to illegally distribute a controlled dangerous substance
- if the non-controlled substance was purchased, whether the amount of the consideration was substantially greater than the reasonable value of the non-controlled substance
- whether the physical appearance of the non-controlled substance is substantially identical to that of a controlled dangerous substance.

It is not a defense to a prosecution under this section that the substance a person possessed or purchased was not a controlled dangerous substance if the person reasonably believed that it was a controlled dangerous substance.

A person who violates this section is guilty of a misdemeanor and on conviction is subject to imprisonment not exceeding 1 year or a fine not exceeding $500.00 or both; Criminal Law Article 5-618.

Drug-Induced Conduct: In this section, "drug" does not include alcohol. A person may not administer a controlled dangerous substance or other drug to another without that person's knowledge and commit against that other;

- a crime of violence as defined in 14-101 of this Article
- a sexual offense in the third degree under 3-307 of this Article.

A person who violates this section is guilty of a misdemeanor and on conviction is subject to imprisonment not to exceed 1 year or a fine not exceeding $2,500 or both. Criminal Law Article 5-624.

Controlled Dangerous Substance Near Schools: A person may not manufacture, distribute, dispense, or possess with intent to distribute a controlled dangerous substance in violation of 5-602 of this subtitle or conspire to commit any of these crimes:

- In a school vehicle, as defined under 11-154 of the Transportation Article
- In, on, or within 1,000 feet of real property owned by or leased to an elementary or secondary educational purposes.
- Subsection A of this section applies whether or not school is in session at the time of the crime; or the real property was being used for purposes other than school purposes at the time of the crime.
- The person who violates this section is guilty of a felony and on conviction is subject to (for the first violation) imprisonment not exceeding 20 years or a fine not exceeding $20,000 or both.
- For each subsequent violation, imprisonment not less than 5 years and not exceeding 40 years or a fine not to exceed $40,000 or both.
- The court may not suspend the 5-year minimum sentence required in this section.
- Except as otherwise provided in 4-305 of the Correctional Service Article a person sentenced under paragraph (1) of this section is not eligible for parole during this period of the 5 year minimum sentence.

- A sentence imposed under paragraph (1) of this subsection shall be consecutive to any other sentence imposed.
- Maps as evidence, in a prosecution under this section, a map or certified copy of a map made by a county or municipal unit to depict the location and boundaries of the area within 1,000 feet of real property owned by or leased to an elementary school, or county board and used for school purposes is admissible as prima facie evidence of the location and boundaries of depicted area. If the governing body of the county or municipal corporation approves the map or certified copy of the map as an official record of the location and boundaries of the depicted area.
- The map or certified copy of the map shall be filed with the county or municipal corporation, which shall maintain the map or the certified copy of the map as an official record.
- The governing body of the county or municipal corporation may revise periodically the map or certified copy of the map.
- This subsection does not preclude the prosecution from introducing other evidence to establish an element of crime under this section.
- This subsection does not preclude the use or admissibility of maps or diagrams other than those approved by the county or municipal corporation. [An. Code 1957, art. 27. 286D; 2002, ch 26, 2]

Unlawfully Distributing Controlled Dangerous Substance: A registrant may not distribute or dispense a controlled dangerous substance listed in Schedule 1 or Schedule II in violation of 5-303 (d) of this title; or distribute a controlled dangerous substance listed in Schedule I or Schedule II in the course of the registrant's legitimate business, except in accordance with an order from under 5-303 (d) of this title.

Penalty, if the trier of the fact specifically finds that a person knowingly or intentionally violated subsection (a) of this section, the person is guilty of a misdemeanor and on conviction is subject to imprisonment not to exceed 2 years or a fine not exceeding $100,000 or both.

- In all other cases, a person who violates subsection (a) (1) of this section is subject to a civil penalty not exceeding $50,000.

- A person who violates subsection (a) (2) of this section is guilty of a felony and on conviction not to exceed 10 years or a fine not exceeding $100,000 or both. [An. Code 1957, art 27, 288 (a), (1), (c), 289 (a), (1) (b); 2002 ch. 26 2.]

5-708. Inhalant: This section applies to fingernail polish, model airplane glue, or any other substance that causes intoxication, inebriation, excitement, stupefaction, or dulling of the brain or nervous system when smelled or inhaled. This section does not apply to the inhalation of an aesthesis for medical or dental purposes; or controlled dangerous substances.

1. A person may not deliberately smell or inhale a substance listed in paragraph (2) of this subsection in an amount that causes intoxication, excitement, stupefaction, or dulling of the brain or nervous system.

2. This section applies to a drug or any other noxious substances or chemical that contains the following:

- an aldehyde
- butane
- butyl nitrite
- a chlorinated hydrocarbon
- ether
- a fluorinated hydrocarbon
- a ketone
- methyl benzene
- nitrous oxide
- an organic acetate
- another substance containing solvents releasing toxic vapors

Penalty, a person who violates this section is guilty of a misdemeanor. On conviction is subject to imprisonment not exceeding 6 months or a fine not exceeding $500 or both. [An. Code 1957, art. 27 301; 2002, ch. 26, 2]

5-709. Distribution of Inhalant and Instruction on Inhaling: In this section "distribute" includes actual, constructive, or attempted transfer, exchange, or delivery, regardless of remuneration or agency relationship.

- A person may not distribute or possess with the intent to distribute to another a substance listed in 5-708 of this subtitle
- With the intent to induce unlawful inhaling of the substance
- With knowledge that the other will unlawfully inhale the substance

A person may not instruct another in the practice of inhaling or smelling that is prohibited under, 5-708 of this subtitle; or distributes a butane canister to a minor.

Penalty- a person who violates this section is guilty of a misdemeanor and on conviction is subject to imprisonment not exceeding 18 months or a fine not exceeding $1,000 or both.

5-605. Keeping Common Nuisance: Common nuisance means a dwelling, building, vehicle, vessel, aircraft, or other place.

- Resorted to by individuals for the purpose of administering illegally controlled dangerous substances
- Where controlled dangerous substances or controlled paraphernalia are manufactured, distributed, dispensed, stored, or concealed illegally.
- Many parents can be charged with this crime if a son or daughter has dangerous substances in the house [An. Code 1957. art.27 289 (a) (5); 2002, ch. 26. 2.]

5-619. Drug Paraphernalia: (A). Factors that determine drug paraphernalia- to determine whether an object is drug paraphernalia, a court shall consider, among other logically relevant factors:

- Any statement by an owner or person in control of the object concerning its use.
- Any prior convention of an owner or a person in control of the object under a State or federal law relating to a controlled dangerous substance.

- The proximity of the object, in time and space, to a direct violation of this section or to a controlled dangerous substance.
- A residue of controlled dangerous substance on the object.
- Direct or circumstantial evidence of the intent of an owner or a person in control of the object to deliver it to another who, the owner or person knows or should reasonably know, intends to use the object to facilitate a violation of this section.
- Any instructions, oral or written, provided with the object concerning its use.
- National and local advertising concerning use of the object.
- The manner in which the object is displayed for sale.
- Whether the owner or person in control of the object is a licensed distributor or dealer of tobacco products or other legitimate supplier of related items to the community.
- Direct or circumstantial evidence of the ratio of sales of the object to total sales of the business enterprise.
- The existence and scope of legitimate use for the object in the community and expert testimony concerning use of the object.

(B). Finding of intention or design – Innocence of owner not dispositive – The innocence of an owner or a person in control of an object as a direct violation of this section does not prevent a finding that the object is intended for use or designed for use as drug paraphernalia.

(C).Use or possession with the intent to use; penalty; medical necessity;

- Unless authorized under this title, a person may not use or possess with intent to use drug paraphernalia to; plant, propagate, cultivate, grow, harvest, manufacture, compound, convert, produce, process, prepare, test, analyze, pack, repack, store, contain, or conceal a controlled dangerous substance.
- Inject, ingest, inhale, or otherwise introduced into the human body a controlled dangerous substance.

116

- A person who violates this subsection is guilty of a misdemeanor and on conviction is subject to for the first violation (I), a fine not to exceed $500.
- For each subsequent violation, imprisonment not exceeding 2 years or a fine not exceeding $2,000 or both.
- A person who is convicted of violating this subsection for the first time and who previously has been convicted of violating subsection (d) (4) of this section is subject to the penalty specified under paragraph (2) (ii) of this subsection.
- In a prosecution under this subsection involving drug paraphernalia related to marijuana, the defendant may introduce and the court shall consider as a mitigating factor any evidence of medical necessity.
- If the court finds that the person used or possessed drug paraphernalia related to marijuana because of medical necessity, on conviction of a violation of this subsection, the maximum penalty that the court may impose on a person is a fine not exceeding $100.00

(D). Delivery or sale; penalty; (Paragraph 1),Unless authorized under this title, a person may not deliver or sell, or manufacture or possess with intent to deliver or sell, drug paraphernalia, knowing, or under circumstances where one reasonably should know, that the drug paraphernalia will be used.

- A person who violates this subsection is guilty of a misdemeanor and on conviction is subject to a fine not to exceed $500.00 for the first offense.
- For each subsequent violation, imprisonment not exceeding 2 years or a fine not exceeding $2,000 or both.

A person who is convicted of violating this subsection for the first time and who previously has been convicted of paragraph (4) of this subsection is subject to imprisonment not exceeding 2 years or a fine not exceeding $2,000 or both.

- (D-4). If a person who is at least 18 years old violates paragraph (1) of this subsection by delivering drug paraphernalia to a minor who is at least 3 years younger that the person, the person is guilty of a separate misdemeanor and on conviction is subject to imprisonment not exceeding 8 years or a fine not exceeding $15,000

(E). Advertising; Penalty, - A person may not advertise in a newspaper, magazine, handbill, poster, sign, mailing, or other writing or publication, or by sound tract, knowing, or under circumstances where one reasonably should know, that the purpose of the advertisement, wholly or partly, is to promote the sale or delivery of drug paraphernalia.

- A person who violates this subsection is guilty of a misdemeanor and on conviction is subject to for the first time, a fine not to exceed $500.00. For each subsequent violation, imprisonment not to exceed 2 years or a fine not exceeding $2,000 or both.

5-905. Repeat Offenders: In general, - A person convicted of a subsequent crime under this title is subject to;

- A term of imprisonment twice that otherwise authorized;
- Twice the fine otherwise authorized or both.
- Rule of interpretation, - For purpose of this section, a crime is considered a subsequence crime, if before the conviction for the crime, the offender has ever been convicted of a crime under this title or under any law of the United States or of this or any other relating to other controlled dangerous substance.
- Superseded laws – Parole, probation, suspension of sentence – A person convicted of a subsequent crime under a law superseded by this is eligible for parole, probation, and suspension of sentences in same manner as theses persons convicted under this title.
- Sentencing in conjunction with other sentences- a sentence on a single count under this section may be imposed in conjunction with other sentences under this title. [An. Code 1957, art. 27 293; 2002, ch. 26, 2]

DUI and DWI Laws Are in
The Alcohol Section of This Book

Chapter Six
The Enabler

The Enabler

There is an old saying, "Behind every good man, there is a good woman". Behind every alcoholic and drug user, there is a father, mother, wife, or husband hoping to change the person whom they love so dearly. And let's not forget the children, the co-workers, neighbors, and friends that have made an impact on their lives. As parents, we have this idea that we can fix anything; and then things will be better, …things will be OK. Well things don't get better; you can't help someone who doesn't want help, no matter how hard you try and no matter how much you love them.

As a parent of an addicted son, I also thought just like you. After all, I was a retired narcotic agent who taught drug and alcohol classes. I could spot a user a mile away. However, when it came to my own son, I was as blind as a bat. I never realized that I was an enabler. I just thought I was fixing things, fixing the things in my son's life that he couldn't fix. I paid his bills, I signed for loans, I even put my house up for collateral for larger loans, I bought Christmas presents and birthday presents and put his name on them so that family members would think he was the one who bought the gifts, and when all was said and done, my son still had his addiction and I was on my way to the poor house. I felt beat-up and depressed. I thought I was fixing things, but what I was doing was making things worse, worse for him and making life miserable for myself.

People who deal with addictions will fall into three major categories. First there is the kind and loving parent or spouse who just wants to help the addict. They know all about the addiction and understand it. These people have emotionally put a distance between them and the addict so they can be of real help. The addict does not manipulate them and they have no problem stick-

120

ing to the facts. I always tell parents that anger is control and conversation is fact. Most addicts want to control, but what the parent, spouse, or friend needs to do is stick with the facts and if alcohol or drugs are being abused, the person abusing them has a problem, that is a fact.

The next group is the enablers; an enabler is defined as "people who prevent the alcoholic or addict from experiencing their consequences of their disease.

These people are for the most part logical and motivated. However, the time frame of recovery is on their terms and not that of the addict. We see this happen with sports personalities that have addiction problems. A coach may have a player that has a drinking problem, the player promises to stop drinking and go to rehab in the off season. As long as he is producing for the team his actions are tolerated. As soon as his performance declines, he is traded or he retires. If he is arrested for DUI the team bails him out and provides a chauffeur for him.

Next is the employer or the boss. He has an excellent salesman, program manager, engineer or finance person who is producing and contributing to the bottom line. The employer will tolerate the long lunches, missed afternoons, and skipped meetings. Then, when the project is over or the corporate political winds shift, the employee is let go. To avoid any possible litigation, the person is let go due to downsizing, or corporate restructuring.

Next example of an enabler is the spouse. This is someone, regardless of gender, who has become accustomed to a life style made possible by the addicts earning power or popularity. They are used to the vacations, social functions, and the like. So what if the addicted person makes a fool of themselves, "He's had one too many".

The spouse will continue supporting the addict as long as the income or social status remains. Once the alcoholic becomes too much of a burden, the spouse leaves. Their justification is, "I did it for his own good" or, "I did it for the children".

As mentioned in the beginning, the enablers are logical people. If they believe the alcoholic or addict can be rescued, they weigh the cost and benefits. Most people who have family members in 28-day programs feel that they are cured in that period of time. However, what you really have is an insurance company that says "That's all we can pay".

The final category is the codependent. We are not talking about the caring or nursing type of codependency. Rather, we are talking about those people who have their own neurotic psychological addictions. In other words, the addict is their drug of choice. They can be just as manipulative as the drunk and without having any chemical impairment, be very convincing. They control when and how the addict is treated. Often times they will sabotage the recovery by taking the alcoholic or addict out of treatment.

Should the alcoholic or addict be successful in their treatment and recovery, the codependent is now faced with the dilemma of their own addiction.

*I would like to thank Mr. Scott McCann for most of the information and research in his report (above) "What are Enablers?"

Being the enabler and codependent person, is almost being like the phoenix; a bird in Egyptian mythology that lived in the desert for 500 years and then consumed itself by fire, later to rise renewed from its ashes. Because the enabler and codependent person have this desire to continue helping someone struggling with alcohol or drugs, has put them in a new category of human existence. Their lives are filled with hope and dreams that seem to be consumed by fire one day and hope the next.

*Some of the following information comes from the friends and families of the codependent enablers. Who would of ever know that somewhere deep down inside you there lingered a desire to become completely miserable? You must love misery because look at all the things you put up with being a friend or spouse to an alcoholic or drug user! Why?

Because you are an enabler, and enabling allows you to stay in a relationship because your fear of being alone is greater than the experience of your spouse's addictive behavior. You depend on your spouse so much that you enable him / her to continue the addiction, thereby, making you a codependent. Once codependent, your life is no longer yours but becomes enmeshed with the addicts. YOU are just as sick as they are and will probably have to attend some sort of self-help meeting, or subject yourself to years of counseling in order to regain any resemblance of normal life. YOU don't believe me? Ask any other professional or member of a self-help group.

As a parent, I gave because I loved my son. I never knew I was codependent I just thought I was doing the right thing. And I was the most miserable person on earth. As for my son, he never got the help he needed until he lost everything job, home, car, I mean everything. It was after he hit rock bottom things began to change. And after I stopped giving and doing for him, I began to change. Remember, some people can put up with more than other people; but if you're feeling miserable everyday of your life you may need to do the following.

Determine how much you are willing to take and set the boundaries. Talk things over with the family or your friends and make these boundaries clear to everyone. Sticking to your guns will be difficult at times. But you must separate yourself if you're truly going to help the person. Do this in a way that feelings will not be hurt. Remember, anger is control and conversation is fact. Base your boundaries on YOUR decisions NOT on what people think. Caring is not wrong, but you must determine for yourself what you want your life to be about. If the addict has no money or home to live in, he or she may have to re-evaluate his or her life. However, I have found that addicts still use even when extreme threats are made. Consequences and threats may facilitate a change, but true change occurs when the addict decides it is of value to do so. IT IS entirely the addict's choice to use drugs or alcohol.

There are two aspects of change and both of these aspects depend on the person using drugs or alcohol. First, the alcohol or drug user MUST decide that they want change.

You cannot change someone else. If the addict refuses change he or she may feel there's no problem; educators call this the "denial phase". Does the user really know what he or is using? "Yes" and they can manipulate and deceive us in getting their next fix.

It's all about value and what the addict chooses to accept or reject in his or her mind. What the addict is saying to us is, "I am not stopping".

Second, the alcoholic or drug user has to think they can change? The user has got to believe their life will be improved by stopping their addictive behavior. As of today, my son Joshua has almost six-months of clean time. He knows he can impact the lives of others by telling his story and by making new friends. He is also attending college and has helped me co-author this book. I keep him as busy as I can; but the question that I ask myself-everyday when he doesn't stop by, "Where is Josh and what is he doing?" I know that he could relapse at anytime.

I was an enabler and I was also codependent. My son's problems became my drug of choice. Today, I am just like the recovering addict, I take one day at a time and I try to stay focused. Will I ever go back being an enabler? No! Not after the research I did on enablers and codependents. If my son decides to go back into drugs, he will suffer the consequences for his actions.

Alcoholism: A disorder characterized by the excessive consumption of alcoholic beverages, leading to psychological and impaired social and vocational functioning. Also called alcohol abuse alcohol dependence.

Substance abuse: The overindulging and a dependence on an addictive substance, especially alcohol or a narcotic drug. Also called chemical abuse.

Tips for the parents, friends, and family members: The drug addict is well known for their lies and manipulations tactics. The following tips may help you to deal with the addiction problem.

- Never let the addicted person get the upper hand.
- Never give cash to the addicted person to pay a bill or to buy food.
- Never leave the addicted person in your home alone.

- Always check the addict's story out before you make a decision.
- Check the mileage on the family vehicle after it has been used, then ask questions.
- Never believe what a drug addicts tells you, they are well know for their lies and manipulation.
- Always check on medication your in the home; count the pills and check the pill count before the addict leaves your home.
- Know before any conversation with an addict that he or she will become angry if they are backed into a corner.
- Remember the addict must want help before he or she can get help.
- When an addict tells you he or she is going into a treatment program and needs money, check out the story and go with them to pay for the treatment if possible.
- Always remember anger is control and conversation is fact, so stick with the facts.
- Remember the addict will always blame others for their problems.
- Never take an addict to buy his or her drugs, if you do and the police stop you and drugs are found in the car both of you will be arrested. And your family vehicle could be seized.
- Remember when the addict's birthday comes around it would be better off to take them to a good dinner than to buy them new clothes or give them money. Why? Because they will sell the clothes and spend the money on their addictions.
- Never leave piggy banks or money in plain view of an addict.
- If the addicted person has a key to your home get it back. You must make rules as to the time your going to bed and make it clear the doors will be locked.
- If an addict still has a ring or watch that you gave to them get it back and put it away; because they will sell it for the drug of choice when the opportunity arises.

- Remember the addict must change people, places, and things if they expect to recover.
- After treatment, make the person earn back his or her trust. Most treatment programs only last for a few days or weeks. The desire for the drug is still with them and the fight is an everyday battle. Giving them money or presents after treatment could hinder their recovery, so move slowly in this area.
- Go to some meetings with the person in recovery if they ask you. If they don't ask don't be offended.
- Don't ever think the addict will never go back to his or her old ways. It could happen, in fact it happens every day to someone.
- Don't be the taxi cab driver; let the recovering addict work out his or her own problems.
- And most importantly never give up on your child, wife, husband, or friend. You must do what ever it takes to save their life.

Rehabilitation and Treatment

Years ago many people thought that addicts were incurable. Once hooked always hooked, recovery was out of the question, to put it simply there was no road back to a normal life. Many addicts do return to their past demons (drugs of choice) some as soon as they walk out of the doors of treatment programs, for others it may be weeks, months, or even years. However, not all addicts fall back into their old way of life, some do succeed.

A well-rounded treatment program should include, not only controlled detoxification in a hospital environment, but also psychiatric evaluation and therapy, and continued medical supervision and counseling upon the addict's return to the community. The problems addicts face today is having the insurance to pay for treatment. If the addict has no insurance then he or she must come up with the money for a treatment program.

Initial detoxification of addicted persons is best accomplished only under medical supervision in a hospital setting.

However, I have known many people who have suffered through withdraw without being under a doctor's supervision. From what I have been told, it is the pain of withdraw that addicts dread. Many people think that after a person goes through this withdraw that he or she is cured; the pain of withdraw may be gone but the desire for the drug will always be there. This is why the addict must change people, places and things if they ever plan to recover from their addiction to drugs.

Any person not getting the proper help for their addiction problem may never know how to fight the other demons in their life, such as underlying mental and emotional disorders. After proper detoxification and after the addict demonstrates the ability to cope with stressful situations in a protected environment, he or she can return to the community. THIS is the most critical period in the abuser's rehabilitation. IF the abuser does not have that special help from professionals, it will only be a matter of time before the temptation of drug use is knocking at their door.

If we were honest about who gets into treatment programs we would have to say the insured and the wealthy. I know by making this statement that some treatment providers will disagree. Some will tell you there is help out there; all you have to do is find it. I put that theory to a test one day. I had a parent in my office that was trying to get help for her son who had an addiction to heroin. I had her call on her cell phone a treatment program; she was to ask if someone could help her son. She told the intake person that her son had no insurance or money to pay for the treatment. She was advised that there were no beds available. And to make matters worse she was also told that there was a waiting list and it would take two or three weeks for her to even get an appointment. After a few moments I then called from my office phone the same treatment program. I spoke to the same intake provider that the parent spoke to; I told them I had insurance and I needed to get into a program. I was advised by the intake person to come into the office right away that they did have a bed and they would be happy to take care of me. To take my investigation to the next level, I had my son call from his home that same treatment program and tell them he had no insurance but did have the money to pay for his treatment. He was also advise to come into the office and they would be glad to help him.

So where do these people go for help? I thought about this problem for years and came up with the idea of opening a self-help program. I was already teaching a State certified social drinkers program for Maryland, I was qualified as an expert witness in the Federal and State Courts in drugs and alcohol abuse. I had my degree in counseling and thought this would be a good idea to help the ones who had no money or insurance to pay for treatment. I never intended to replace any treatment programs; I am now and always have always been 100% for treatment, I only wanted to provide a service for the indigent or uninsured that were being turned away from treatment programs because they had no funds. Well...I must have offended some of pirates that were flying the flag of a treatment programs. There were some people who never wanted this program to start. In fact, a state official came to my office after I requested a meeting about this new program; I thought he would be excited to hear the good news but I was wrong. I was questioned about the social drinkers program that I had been teaching for Maryland for about ten years and then questioned about my qualifications. After he could find NO issues with the state program or my qualifications he looked me in the eyes and said, "YOU will never get state approval for a drug program in this area."

This guy had no idea what people were going through in this community; people were losing their jobs and insurance, others were living off of their parents. This man's rudeness and arrogance was overwhelming to me, and the witness I had in my office. After his departure the Alpha Program opened that day. Our slogan, "We never turn people away". I'll let you be the judge as to whether this program helps people or not.

The Alpha Program
1799 Merritt Blvd. Dundalk Md. 21222
Thursday Evenings 5-6, 6-7, 7-8 PM
We are inside the Merritt Park Baptist Church
410-288-1399

- A treatment like program for the uninsured, where we never turn people away because of finances.
- The Alpha Programs pays for everyone who wants to get his or her GED.
- The Alpha Program provides counseling free to clients.
- The Alpha Program finds jobs for people who are out of work.
- The Alpha Program does drug and alcohol testing for $2.00 -$10.00
- Classes for the Alpha Program are only $10.00 per session.
- The Alpha Program has used it's money to pay for medication for students.
- The Alpha Program provides food for students who are hungry.
- The Alpha Program has a 24-hour counseling service free to students.
- The Alpha Program has paid for treatment to Dr. Hayes addiction program.
- The Alpha Program has used it's money to bury a student who died from a heroin overdose after we found out his family has no life insurance.
- The Alpha Program had a Thanksgiving Dinner for all the students on Thanksgiving Day along with a father-son football game; there was no cost for the students. One of the student's children said "I am glad my mom was arrested, now we can have a Thanksgiving Dinner." Fifty-four people attended.
- The Alpha Program has an anger management class.
- The Alpha Program has students who help each other with reading and special needs. Some even request to stay in the program after they have completed the 26 weeks of education and counseling just to help others.
- Lawyers use the Alpha Program to help clients that have financial problems.
- Some Judges have agreed to let clients stay in the program because it meets the needs of the client.

- There has never been a complaint made on any staff member from the Alpha Program. Why? Because we treat people the way they should be treated.
- The Alpha Program has formed a softball team to play other treatment programs.
- Soon the men and women in the Alpha Program will open their own company for home improvements. They will run the business and have advisors from the community to help them in decision-making; they will have an opportunity to become productive in the community.
- The Alpha Program has summer picnics for students at no cost to them.
- The Alpha program encourages families to attend the program together, because addiction is a family disease.
- This program saves the State of Maryland thousands of dollars in court time and salary.
- 100% of the students finishing the program without being violated from the courts.
- The Alpha Program try's to get people into treatment programs that need it.

But here's the kicker, the State of Maryland would rather spend thousands of dollars of your tax money sending the indigent back to court for violation of probation because they are not in a treatment program. What is a person to do? The Alpha Program helps so many people and it costs the State nothing. These programs can be set up to help the people who do not have money for treatment. I know it's only a band-aid on a major cut, but for what we are spending in the courts alone just on probation violations we could print material for these programs. I want to make myself very clear, I am 100% for treatment; I am NOT trying to replace any treatment program with this program. My only goal is to help the people who DO NOT have funds for treatment.

So what can you do?
- Call or write the Governor of Maryland and tell him that we need the Alpha Program for the uninsured.
- Call or write your Congressman and tell them how much

the Alpha Program is needed.

- Call or write your Senators and tell him or her we need programs to help the uninsured.
- If you would like to start a program in your church or school contact me and I will help you set-up a program just like the Alpha Program. Your cost is nothing, just your time and the desire to help other is all that is needed.
- As of March 4, 2004 I have not received a response to a letter that I sent to the Governor of Maryland about the Alpha Program. I requested that this program be use as an alternate to treatment for the uninsured or the people who have no funding for a treatment program.
- It is now May 25, 2004. I have been given the run around about getting the Alpha Program Certified as an alternative to treatment. However, the state did pay for one mans in house treatment because he had no funds. I consider that a real victory in it's self. If the state can pay for one man's treatment, then I feel they can pay for others, and I will provide everyone with this information who calls or write me about the state paying for a program for your son, daughter or family member. Remember the key is NOT to give up.

Or you may wish to make a donation to help others:

There are so many who need help that have addiction problems; Dr, Hayes has a great program to help people with the withdraw; the cost for his program is about $200.00 he provides medication to the addict so they can get through the sickness of withdraw. There are others who need medication, clothes, housing, bus passes, shoes, and jobs. Some even want to get into a GED program. If you wish to make a donation to help a person on drugs, make your check payable to:

Alpha Program in care of
Merritt Part Baptist Church
1799 Merritt Blvd. Baltimore 21222
or Call 410-288-1399

Your gift will go to help a person who has a drug problem
Remember, "We never turn people away"

Chapter Seven
The Hiding Place For Drugs
General Questions About Drugs

Hiding The Drugs

I often hear parents tell me, "I know where my son hides his drugs"; well you may want to read this chapter very carefully. This is the chapter that will help you, the parent, locate the hidden drugs in your home. It is very important that you, the parent, understand one thing, YOU CAN BE ARRESTED if the police find drugs in your home.

<u>Person</u>:
Artificial limbs
Baby diapers
Batter box or hearing aid
Belts- split zippers or buckles
Buttocks
Canteens
Casts
Cigar holders
Cigarette lighters, filters and packs
Collar stays
Compacts
Contact lens cases
Corsets
Cuffs and wristbands
Earrings
Ears- inside and behind
Film cans
Foreskin or penis
Glass eyes
Hair – processed, buns and wigs
Handkerchiefs

Hatbands
Hollow end of cane
Inhalers
Inside fly flap of trousers
Jewelry
Jock straps
Lapels
Lining of clothing and change purse
Lipstick tube
Locket
Luggage
Match box and books
Money belts
Mouth
Nose
Pens
Personal bags
Pill vials
Pipe stems
Pockets
Rectum
Rings
Sanitary napkins or tampons
Self addressed envelopes
Shoes
Socks
Sticks or gum
Swallowed with string tied to teeth
Taped under breast and brassiere
Taped between toes and feet
Thermos jugs
Ties
Tobacco tin and pouches
Umbrella handles
Under false teeth
Band-Aids

Bandages
Uniform shoulder patches and badges
Vagina
Wrist watch-inside and back
Wallets
Home:
Aerosol cans
Agitator of washer
Air-conditioning register
Antenna and base of television
Art kits
Attic insulation
Band-aid boxes
Base of lamps
Bathtub legs and lips
Batteries
Behind baseboards, medicine box, mirrors, picture frames
posters wall phones and walls
Bedposts
Books
Cameras
Ceiling tiles
Cellar beams
Chandelier
Chessmen
Child's bank
Closet
Clothesline pole
Clothing gloves, shoes, sleeves
Cookies and candy
Dog collars and house
Dolls
Doorknobs
Douche bags
Electrical sockets
False bottoms of fish tanks radiator covers

False ceilings and chimneys
Fire alarm bell
Fire hose
Flashlights
Flowerpots
Florescent light tube
Footlockers
Furniture upholstery
Fuse box
Garbage bags
Hanging out windows
Hollow closet rods, curtain rods, eggs, fruit, vegetables, furni-
ture, Holy Bible, soap
Hung behind curtains
Inside ironing board legs, newspapers, radios, televisions and
wigs
Kitchen canisters and containers
Light switches
Loaves of bread
Magazines
Magnet boxes
Mailboxes
Mattresses
Musical instruments and cases
Pens
Pet boxes
Pillowcases
Prescription bottles
Razor blade dispensers in older houses
Record albums
Refrigerator butter, meat trays, fruit, ice cubes, and vegetables
Salt and pepper shakers
Sealed cigarette packs
Shaving brush handles
Shoe polish containers
Sink traps

Stick deodorant containers
Talcum containers
Taped in dresser and behind drawers
Tea bags
Telephone base and coin slots
Toaster trays
Toilet bowl, tanks, and paper
Top of window, doorsills and molding
Toys and games
Trophies
Under washbowl
Under carpet
Vaseline jars
Venetian blinds
Wall ceiling fixtures
Window ledge of neighbor
Wax paper dispensers
Window shade

Automobile:

Air and oil filters
Armrest
Ashtrays
Behind back seat, bumpers, head lights, and tail lights
Carburetor
Cigarette lighter
Convertible tops
False battery
Bottom of trunk bed
Dual mufflers
Gas tanks
Heaters
Heater hoses
Floorboards
Frame
Fuse box of trunk
Gas tank inside on string

Glove compartment

Heater hide a key

Hollow voltage regulator

Hood insulation

Hubcaps

Inside horn

Instrument panel

License plates

Motorcycle handlebars

Oil cap

Picnic jug in trunk

Pill vials

Radio speaker

Roof and surfboard racks

Seats

Shift knobs

Spare tire

Sun visors

Tail pipes

Taxi roof lights

Tied to axle

Trunk

Under break pedal, chrome, foot pedal rugs, and side fenders

Vents air and heat

Window channel

Windshield washer bag

General Questions About Drugs

What is a drug?

A drug is a substance that has an effect upon the body or mind.

What is drug dependence?

Drug dependence is a state of psychological or physical dependence or both, which results from chronic, periodic, or continuous use. Many kinds of drug dependence exist; they all have special problems associated with them. Not everyone who uses a mind –altering chemical becomes dependent upon it. Alcohol is one common example of this point. The majority of persons who drink do not harm themselves or those around them. However, millions of Americans are dependent on alcohol.

What is addiction?

Addiction is physical dependence upon a drug. Their scientific definitions include the development of tolerance and withdraw. As a person develops tolerance he requires larger and larger amounts of the drug to produce the same effect.

When the addicted person stops using the drug abruptly, the period of withdraw is characterized by such distressing symptoms as vomiting and convulsions. A compulsions to repeat the use of the addicting drug is understandable because the drug temporarily solves one's problems and keeps the withdraw symptoms away.

A person can have an addiction to sedatives and certain tranquilizers as well as narcotics. Drug dependence of any kind is a serious problem for the individual and society.

Questions About Drugs

Are all drugs harmful?

Every drug is harmful when taken in excess. Some drugs can also be harmful if taken in dangerous combinations with other drugs. Our society must develop a new respect for all drugs. This would include prescription drugs as well as over the counter drugs.

Why are drugs being abused these days?

Drug use is not a new phenomenon in the United States. One of the most alarming comments that people share with me is that they are bored with life. Others tell me that they are frustrated or depressed and look for an escape from reality. These drugs do not produce any improvement for the problem; rather, it is a flight from the problems.

What is meant by a drug culture?

A drug culture or subculture is a group of people whose lives are committed to drugs. The members of any subculture may congregate in a particular geographic area, for example while working in undercover narcotics we knew the users and dealers would congregate in Patterson Park. Today they are found in clubs and in our schools.

Do drug abusers take more than one drug at a time?

People who abuse one drug will most likely abuse all sorts of drugs. Some have stated they are looking for a new "high". Some people have played chemical roulette by taking everything, including unidentified pills. However, in heroin or other narcotic addictions the users will stay pretty much with that drug, but will always seek a way to enhance their high. An example of this was shared with me in a counseling session. The young man who I was counseling stated, "I went to the police department parking lot during shift change last night and fired heroin into my arm just to enhance my high." The addicted person is always looking for ways to enhance their high; this young man felt that if he used his drug of choice in front of the police officers and did not get caught his high would be enhanced.

Why do some affluent people become involved in drug usage?

Eliminating poverty does not eliminate drug abuse. Some athletes have used drugs to enhance their skills; however, instead of helping them, the drugs destroyed them. When a person no longer needs to work in order to eat and clothe himself, he may develop problems of leisure. If he has no motivation or drive to create viable goals, he may become bored or alienated, and vulnerable to the temptation of using chemical substances for productive living.

Can the effects of drug abuse be passed on to the unborn?

Some babies born to heroin-addicted mothers have shown withdraw systems. It is always best to consult with your doctor during a pregnancy, advise him / her as to what drugs have been abused and he / she should be able to advise you on the possibility of any problems that can be passed on to the new born because of abuse.

Where does one go if he or she is becoming or is dependent upon drugs?

First and foremost, the user MUST want help in order to get help. In Maryland I have found that the Hudson House in Salisbury has one of the best programs that I have ever encountered. The staff is all very friendly and go out of their ways to make both the user and the family feel comfortable. They do take insurance and will answer all questions presented to them. If a person has no insurance, the Alpha Program in Dundalk,

Maryland is a self-help outpatient program that works just like a treatment program without the high cost. AA meetings and NA meeting can also be a helpful tool for the addicted person. You may check with your insurance company to see what your policy limits are and then call the department of health and locate a program that is near you.

What can a parent do to help a child who is abusing dangerous drugs or narcotics?

Try and open communication line with the person; seek counseling and treatment if possible. Try not to be judgmental or negative, remember anger is controlling but communication is fact. Never give up on your son or daughter. A drug and alcohol addiction is a family problem. Each solution to a drug or alcohol problem must be individualized, what works for one person may not work for another.

Is it possible to obtain help without including legal penalties?

A person who wants help should understand one important fact; is he getting help because he is in trouble or because he really wants help. If the person has a legal problem, he or she must deal with the legal issues regardless of the help they receive. Doing something about the drug or alcohol problem is a positive thing when one stands before a judge in a criminal case.

What more can be done to curb the misuse of drugs?

Get involved with your kids, do family activities together. Ask questions to your kids like a reporter seeks a story in the hometown newspaper; who, what, where, when, why, and how. That should cover it and when you think you have asked all the questions ask them again. Check on your kids and even look in the room when you clean. I know, some of you will say my son or daughter needs their privacy. Your right but if you child is using drugs let them know they have no privacy. I always tell parents. "I can't talk to a grave marker once you're gone." Be a parent first then a friend.

143

What sort of programs could make an impact on my son or daughters life?

Life is filled with lessons; the funeral home is a place where everyone learns just how short life really is. I have had forty-four of my students that have died because of drug and alcohol addictions and I always make it a point to ask young people to accompany me to the funeral home; there they can see first hand the pain of addiction.

Scared straight programs are also very good, however, you must be court ordered to attend these programs. NA and AA are good meetings to attend, they have good speaker and can influence the way our children think. In addition, education and prevention classes are great tools to help our children.

When communication breaks down, what should I do?

Always stay cool, getting upset only adds fuel to the already out of control fire. If the son or daughter is using drugs, then YOU must do what ever it takes to save their life. Get the facts and never assume. Start taking privileges away and stick by your decisions. If a child is living under your roof, he or she should be living by your rules.

Many drug users have told me that they will upset the family and display anger just so the family would leave them alone. Remember, anger is controlling and communication is fact. Whenever a drug user gets upset they are trying to control the situation and in most cases they will if you let them.

Can a parent be arrest if the son / daughter keeps their drugs in the house?

The answer is simple, "YES". You as a parent can be charged with operating and maintaining a disorderly house. If the police find drugs in your family car you may also lose your transportation. And if the police find enough drugs in the family car you may never get your vehicle back, and YOU must make the payments on a car you no longer own if you have a lien on it; because the bank will not sign off on property seized in a drug arrest.

What can I do if I know someone is selling drugs?

You can call the narcotics division and give the information to them over the phone. You do not have to give your name. Or write all the information down and send it to the narcotic division. The police department narcotics division is always looking for information. If you wish you may send a copy to the Maryland State Police and mark on the envelope supervisor of the narcotics division.

Should I turn my son into the police if I find drugs?

The first thing you must remember is that you are trying to save your child's life. You must do whatever it takes even if it means having them arrested. However, you must understand that this may cause you money for an attorney and bail if it is required. So, I would consult with your family attorney first and follow their instructions. Many parents have different thoughts about this issue, what to do or what not to do.

Can I be arrested if someone has drugs in the car I am riding in?

It would depend on where the drugs are found. If drugs are found inside the car and not on a person the answer is "YES". If the drugs are found in a person's pocket or on the person then the answer is "NO". However, it depends on the officer making the arrest. Sometimes everyone is transported to the police station if the investigation has been on going.

Who gets arrested when a house is hit with a search warrant?

As a general rule everyone in the house goes to jail. It also depends on what the search warrant is for. Almost always in drug warrants the police have already made a drug buy from someone in the house before the search warrant is signed by a judge and issued to the officers.

Is it true that police officers must knock on someone's door before they come into the house with a search warrant?

The law is very clear on serving of a search warrant. The officer or law enforcement officer must knock on a door before entering into a house. However, I have been told that the law does not say how loud a law enforcement officer must knock before he enters into the house. Is a light tap on a defendant's door a "knock"? To some officer's the answer is "yes", and for some defendants the answer is "no".

Does being arrested mean I am going to jail?

"NO" being arrested just means you are going to be detained for a period of time. You may be released without spending any time in jail. Police officer's do not sentence you jail, only the judge can do that. However, if they have a warrant out on you then "Yes" you will be going to jail until your court date or until you post bail. A police officer "CAN" hold you for a number of hours or days if he or she believes you are or could be a suspect in that case. In addition, the police officer can hold you in custody if you refuse to or "CANNOT" properly identify who you really are.

How much will my bail be if I am arrested?

Your cost for bail is 10% of the bail. An example of this is if you have a bail put on you for $4,000 your bail is $400.00. If you have never been arrested you most likely will not have a bail put on you. You may be released on your "own recognizance's"; this means you post no threat for not showing up for court. If you are a homeowner you may put up your property for the bail. However, if you do this for a family member or friend and they do not show up for court "you" could lose your home.

When do I call an attorney?

You have the right to have an attorney present with you before any questions are asked to you. The police officer should read your rights to you when you are arrested. He or she will then permit you to call your attorney. Remember, anything you say or do can be used against you in a court of law. So if you are not sure, call your attorney.

If I decide to work with the police as an informant will it help me?

If you decide to work with the police as an informant (one who provides information to police) and you have a pending case with the officers, work out the details and have it signed by some one in the State's Attorney Office. As a retired narcotic officer, I promised a defendant that I would help him in court; my intentions where good, but the setting judge in the case refused to help the defendant, this made me look like I lied to the defendant and the bond of trust was lost.

If all parties in the case agree, there should never be a problem for someone in the State's Attorney Office to give to you a signed document outlining the agreement. You may even have your attorney work out the details if you feel more comfortable.

You may have information about a crime that has taken place, and you are faced with a criminal charge yourself you may have a way out. Police officers work together, your information could be just what they are looking for in solving unsolved cases.

Even if you have traffic charges, talk to the officer tell him what you would like to do. NEVER give the information first; and if the charging officer says "no" call the detectives and ask them to help you they in return will contact the charging officer and work things out. You may be very surprised as to what you can do with the information you think is worthless.

Will DUI arrest always stay on my driving record?

If you have been charged with a DUI, regardless what happens in court, the charge will always show up on your driving record. The points will come off after two years but the charge of DUI will never come off your driving record. Why? Because this is how Maryland tracks DUI offenders. If your getting a driving record from the MVA ask for a "court copy" of your record, this is the history of your driving.

Can I have my criminal record expunged?

"YES" criminal records can be expunged. However, consult with your attorney because there is a lot of paper work that you must file. There are some charges that cannot be removed from your arrest record; your attorney will advise you.

Chapter Eight
Alcohol

Alcohol

Alcohol is the number one drug abused today; in this chapter you will learn the facts about alcohol. The following questions are used in our state certified alcohol education program; take time and answer each question. The answers to all questions are also found in this chapter. Use notebook paper for your answers.

1. Define in your own words what alcohol looks like. Take a moment to think this question out carefully. There are no right or wrong answers.
2. What is the first thing that comes to mind when you hear these words, problem drinker, treatment program, drunk, AA meetings.
3. Is alcoholism an illness? If you answer yes, explain how a person gets this illness. If you answer no, explain why you think alcoholism is just a behavior.
4. How much alcohol does a person drink in order to be an alcoholic?
5. What contains more alcohol? 1oz of 100 proof whiskey, 4oz of wine, or 12oz of beer.
6. When you hear these words *drunk driver*, what is the first thing that comes to your mind?
7. Who is arrested more for DUI men or women?
8. Is it safe to use medication with alcohol? Explain your answer.
9. Make a list of ways you can identify a drunk who is driving on a public highway.
10. How many people do you think die every year on U.S. highways due to drinking and driving?
11. If you were the judge, what would you do with the person who has committed the following alcohol violations? Arrested for their drunk driving offense, arrested for their

second drunk driving offense, arrested for their third drunk driving offense.

12. Do you think all people should go to jail for drinking and driving?

13. What do you think other countries do with drunk drivers?

14. Can habitual alcohol dependency cause brain damage? Explain your answer.

15. Why do you think advertising is important to the owners of breweries?

16. List five reasons why you think people drink alcohol.

17. What is a responsible drinker?

18. What is a non-responsible drinker?

19. Make a list of problems that drinking may cause in our society.

20. Make a list of problems that a family may have if someone they love is an alcoholic.

21. How much do taxpayers spend on social welfare benefits in one year because of alcohol problems?

22. How much does the United States spend on crime investigation because of alcohol abuse in a one-year period?

23. Maryland Law: what are the administrative penalties that the Motor Vehicle Administration could impose on a person that has been arrested for DWI or DUI?

24. Make a list of myths about how a person can sober up.

25. What is a BAL or BAC?

26. What tests are available to determine a BAL or BAC?

27. Put a figure on the amount of loses to companies because of employee alcohol abuse.

28. Make a list of the possible cost you could incur if you are arrested for DUI.

29. Explain the fetal alcohol syndrome.

30. What is the chemical formula for alcohol?

31. What kind of alcohol do we drink?

32. What are some of the symptoms of the final stages of alcoholism?

33. Make a list of the medical effects on the body when a person is a heavy user of alcohol.

34. Describe what is meant by, being in denial.
35. Describe what a hangover is.
36. How does alcohol effect the stomach?
37. How does alcohol effect the liver?
38. What are some of the consequences of alcohol abuse or addiction?
39. How does alcohol affect the brain?
40. How does alcohol distort eye focus?
41. Explain the route that alcohol travels in the body. Starting right after the person takes his or her first swallow of alcohol.
42. What does the word detoxification mean?
43. Explain what an enabler does.
44. Name some inpatient programs for alcohol or drug treatment. Do they help people who are uninsured?
45. Explain the operation of an outpatient program?
46. To the alcoholic, what does the word recovery mean?
47. Name three diseases caused by alcoholism.
48. Make a list of things a family can do if they have a loved one addicted to alcohol.
49. List reasons why a person could find it hard to change their behavior in drinking.
50. What action do some alcoholics take to relieve their pain of alcoholism?
51. When should a person get help for his or her alcohol problem?
52. Explain what a skid row alcoholic is.
53. Explain what the Michigan Alcohol Screening Test is.
54. What are the four stages of on the job signs of alcoholism?
55. Can alcoholism be cured?
56. How was alcohol used in the old Wild West?
57. If you are convicted of a DUI, how many point will be put on your driving record?
58. Can the officer search your vehicle after you have been arrested for DUI?
59. Can a person ask for a jury trial if they are arrested for DUI?
60. What is the function of the liver?

Did you know according to MADD?

- 42,815 people were killed in traffic accidents in 2002, 17,419 were killed in alcohol related accidents an average of 1 person every 30 minutes. (NHTSA, 2003)
- In 2001, half a million people were injured in alcohol related accidents. An average of 1 person every 2 minutes. (Bincoe, Seay et. al. 2002)
- Alcohol is closely related to violence; about 40% of all crime, violent and non-violent, are committed under the influence of alcohol. (Bureau of Justice Statistics, 1998)
- The highest prevalence of both binge and heavy drinking in 2000 was for young adults aged 18-25, with the peak rate occurring at age 21. (SAMHSA 2000)
- Alcohol related fatalities are primarily caused by the consumption of beer 80%.
- From fatal crashes from midnight to 3:00AM. 79% involved alcohol. (NHTSA 2001)
- In 2002, motor vehicle crashes were the leading cause of death from people 2-33. (NHTSA 2003)
- Binge drinking has been defined as at least 5 drinks in a row for men and 4 drinks in a row for women. (Wechsler et. al. 2002)

Total traffic fatalities vs. alcohol related traffic fatalities:

- 1982, 26,173 people died in alcohol related accidents; total fatalities for the year were 43,945.
- 1983, 24,635 people died in alcohol related accidents; total fatalities for the year were 42,589
- 1984, 24,762 people died in alcohol related accidents; total fatalities for the year were 44, 257.
- 1985, 23,167 people died in alcohol related accidents; total fatalities for the year were 43,825
- 1986, 25,017 people died in alcohol related accidents; total fatalities for the year were 46,087.
- 1987, 24,094 people died in alcohol related accidents; total fatalities for the year were 46,390.

- 1988, 23,833 people died in alcohol related accidents; total fatalities for the year were 47,087.
- 1989, 22,424 people died in alcohol related accidents; total fatalities for the year were 45,582.
- 1990, 22,587 people died in alcohol related accidents; total fatalities for the year were 44,599.
- 1991, 20,159 people died in alcohol related accidents; total fatalities for the year were 41,508.
- 1992, 18,290 people died in alcohol related accidents; total fatalities for the year were 39,250.
- 1993, 17,908 people died in alcohol related accidents; total fatalities for the year were 40,150.
- 1994, 17,308 people died in alcohol related accidents; total fatalities for the year were 40,716.
- 1995, 17,732 people died in alcohol related accidents; total fatalities for the year were 41,817.
- 1996, 17,749 people died in alcohol related accidents; total fatalities for the year were 42,065.
- 1997, 16,711 people died in alcohol related accidents; total fatalities for the year were 42,013.
- 1998, 16,673 people died in alcohol related accidents; total fatalities for the year were 41,501.
- 1999, 16,572 people died in alcohol related accidents; total fatalities for the year were 41,717.
- 2000, 17,380 people died in alcohol related accident; total fatalities for the year were 41,945.
- 2001, 17,400 people died in alcohol related accidents; total fatalities for the year were 42,196
- 2002, 17,419 people died in alcohol related accidents; total fatalities for the year were 42, 815

Facts about motor vehicle crashes:
- In 1994, alone Federico Peoa, Secretary of Transportation released a new study of the economic impact of motor vehicle crashes on the U.S. economy, detailing a staggering $150.5 billion cost.
- Also, in 1994 we had 40,716 deaths, 5.2 million people

injured in vehicles and 27 million damaged vehicles. This report came from NHTSA 43-96 August 7, 1996.

Effects of alcohol:

- Ethyl alcohol, or ethanol, is a clear, thin, odorless liquid that boils at 173 degrees F (78 degrees C).

- Ethyl alcohol is what we drink, and from now on will be referred to simply as "alcohol".

- Alcohol is produced during a natural process called fermentation, which occurs when yeast, a microscopic plant that floats freely in the air, reacts with sugar in fruit or vegetables juice, creating alcohol and releasing carbon dioxide. The process stops naturally when about 11% to 14% of the juice is alcohol, the product of this fermentation is wine. A similar process is used to make beer.

- Distillation is a process used to make beverages with higher alcohol content. In this process, the fermented liquid is heated until it vaporizes, and then the vapor is cooled until it condenses into a liquid again. Distilled alcoholic beverages (e.g., whiskey, gin, vodka, and rum) contain 40% to 50% alcohol. They are sometimes referred to as spirits or hard liquor.

- When someone drinks an alcoholic beverage it flows into the stomach. While it is in the stomach, the drinker does not feel the effects of the alcohol, but alcohol does not remain in the stomach very long. Some of it is absorbed through the stomach walls into the bloodstream, but most alcohol passes into the small intestine and then into the bloodstream, and circulates throughout the body. Once alcohol is in the bloodstream, it reaches the brain and the drinkers begins to feel its effects. The reason that a large person does not feel the effects of a drink as quick as a small person is because the larger person has more blood and other body fluids and will not have as high a level of alcohol in the blood after drinking the same amount of alcohol.

- The body disposes of alcohol in two ways: elimination and oxidation. Only about 10% of the alcohol in the body

155

leaves by elimination from the lungs and kidneys. About 90% of the alcohol leaves by oxidation.

- The liver plays a major role in the body's oxidation of alcohol. When alcohol enters the liver, some of it is changed to a chemical called acetaldehyde. When acetaldehyde is combined with oxygen, acetic acid is formed. When the acetic acid is further combined with oxygen, carbon dioxide and water are formed.
- The oxidation of alcohol produces calories. One ounce of pure alcohol contains about 163 calories or about 105 calories in a 1- ounce glass of whiskey or gin, but it does not contain vitamins or other physically beneficial nutrients.
- The liver can oxidize only a certain amount of alcohol each minute; the oxidation rate of alcohol in a person weighing 150 pounds, for example, is about 7 grams of alcohol per hour.
- If a person drank no more than 3/4 of an ounce of whiskey or a half a bottle of beer every hour, the alcohol would never accumulate in the body, the person would feel little of the effects of the alcohol, and would not become intoxicated.

The effects of alcohol on an individual depend on a variety of factors. These include:

- How the person feels before drinking. If a person is upset and tense, very excited, sad, nervous, or even extremely happy, he or she may tend to gulp drinks and actually consume more alcohol that planned.
- Some people expect a drink to help them feel relaxed, happy, angry, or sad. Quite naturally, a drink can produce these feelings, how you want to feel helps you feel that way.
- A person having one drink before dinner is not likely to feel the effects of alcohol. But having six drinks before and during dinner means the individual might not make it through dessert.
- This is a critical factor: four drinks in one hour will have an obvious effect on the drinker, but the same four drinks

over a four-hour period will probably have a very slight, if any, effect.

- Some alcoholic beverages have more alcohol in them than others. Beer has about 4.5%, table wines average from 11% to 14%, fortified or dessert wines such as sherry or port have 16% to 20%, and distilled spirits range from 40% to 50%. However, 12 ounces of beer, 5 ounces of wine, and 1-1/2 ounces of distilled spirits contains approximately the same amount of alcohol.

- Because of the way alcohol circulates in the body, the size of the drinker also relates to the effects of alcohol. A person weighing 220 pounds will not feel the effects of a drink as much as a person weighing 120 pounds.

- The alcohol consumed does not effect the drinker until it has been absorbed into the bloodstream. Food in the stomach slows the alcohol's absorption, so that a person who has a drink after eating a meal will feel less effects than a person who has a drink on an empty stomach.

- Some drinking a glass of wine may experience light-headedness the first time, but will probably not experience that effect on subsequent occasions. However, most individuals who drink, know what to expect from various amounts of alcohol because of their prior experience with drinking.

- Alcohol acts directly on the brain, and affects its ability to work. The effects of alcohol on the brain are quite complex, but alcohol is usually classified as a depressant. Judgment is the first function of the brain to be affected; the ability to think and make decisions becomes impaired. As more alcohol is consumed, the motor functions of the body are affected.

- This report on the effects of alcohol came from Gail Gleason Milgram Ed.D (CAS) 1997 fact sheet; this is not the entire report, only parts were used.

Alcohol, drugs, and domestic violence:

There is evidence that shows domestic violence and addiction can be lethal. Hundreds of arrest are made everyday for domestic violence. This is also the most dangerous call for law enforcement to respond to.

Robert Mackey, PhD, C.A.C., DVS, recommends the following action be incorporated in treatment programs for battering, in order of priority

- Instruct and support the alcoholic-batterer in abstaining from alcohol use and violence through direct appeal, and through appropriate treatment modalities (or through legal or formal sanctions such as restraining orders, jobs, jeopardy, ect).
- Confront denial and projection of responsibility.
- Incorporate recovery programs for addiction concomitant with anger management and self-control techniques.
- Address relapse issues common to both problems, such as resentment, self-pity, and self-defeating patterns of behavior.
- Teach assertive communication skills
- Educate all parties on techniques of effective-problem – solving, there by empowering each individual in the system to behave in his or her personal best interest.
- Address the needs of the family system. These are inter-generational problems, and prevention is a primary objective.

Dr. Mackey's suggestions for abusers:
* Seek professional help for addiction and or aggressions control. This may require an involvement in appropriate 12-step meetings and in anger management counseling.
* Understand that both battering (physical and psychological) and addiction are progressive. The longer you deny the problems, the more dangerous they become.
* Resentment, denial, self-pity, and loss of control are characteristic of alcoholism and battering. Be willing to get honest.
* Alcoholism and family violence tend to be inter-generational; be prepare for long-term care. Be supportive and encourage help for your children and family.

Dr. Mackey's suggestions for battered persons:
* Define yourself as a survivor of violence rather than a victim.

* Reach out to support groups; isolation is one of your greatest enemies.
* Trust that ultimately you know what is in your best interest, and act accordingly.
* Realize that you are not the cause of another's behavior; you cannot change someone else, so focus on yourself.
* Develop a safety plan for your children in the event that you need to act quickly. A local domestic violence service can assist you in developing your options and advise you on your rights.

Effects of drinking alcohol:

.04 Speech impairment

.04 Commercial impairment levels

.05 Legal presumption starts

.08 Legal definition of under the influence

.10 Accident curves rises 6X's more likely

.14 You are 20 X's more likely to have an accident

.16 You are 35 X's more likely to have an accident

.20 Stumbling

.30 Vomiting and passing out

.40 Coma

.50 Comma, possible death

.60 Death

Approx. Blood Alcohol Percentage

Drinks	Body Weight					
	100	120	140	160	180	200
1	.04	.03	.03	.02	.02	.02
2	.08	.06	.05	.05	.04	.04
3	.11	.09	.08	.07	.06	.06
4	.15	.12	.11	.09	.08	.08

Alcohol and the liver:

This report comes from the National Institute on Alcohol and Alcoholism No. 19PH 329 January 1993.

- Alcohol liver disease is one of the most serious medical consequences of chronic alcohol use.
- Chronic excessive alcohol use is the single most impor-

tant cause of illness and death from the liver disease (alcoholic hepatitis and cirrhosis) in the United States.

- Normal liver function is essential to life.
- The liver is the largest organ of the body.
- The liver filters circulating blood, removing and destroying toxic substances; it secretes bile into the small intestine to help digest and absorb fats; and it is involved in many of the metabolic systems of the body.
- The liver stores vitamins, synthesizes cholesterol; metabolizes or stores sugars; processes fats; and assembles amino acids into various proteins, some for use within the liver and some for exports.
- The liver controls blood fluidity and regulates blood-clotting mechanisms. It also converts the products of protein metabolizes into urea for excretion by the kidneys.
- There are 3 alcohol-induced liver conditions, fatty liver, alcoholic hepatitis, and cirrhosis.
- In some drinkers, alcohol consumption leads to sever alcoholic hepatitis, an inflammation of the liver characterized by fever, jaundice, and abdominal pain.
- Sever alcoholic hepatitis can be confused with many serious abdominal conditions such as cholecystitis (inflammation of the gall bladder), appendicitis, and pancreatitis.
- The most advanced form of alcohol liver injury is alcoholic cirrhosis.
- Alcohol hepatitis may be fatal but can be reversible with abstinence.
- Alcoholic cirrhosis is often progressive and fatal, it can stabilize with abstinence.
- Complications of advanced liver disease include severe bleeding from distended veins in the esophagus, brain disorders (hepatic encephalopathy), accumulation of fluid in the abdomen (ascites), and kidney failure.
- Up to 100 percent of heavy drinkers shows evidence of fatty liver, an estimated 10-35 percent develop alcoholic hepatitis, and 10 to 20 percent develop cirrhosis.

- In general, patients with alcoholic cirrhosis have been drinking heavily for 10 to 20 years.
- Most death from cirrhosis occur in people ages 40-65.
- Mortality from alcoholic hepatitis during early weeks of treatment is very high.
- Treatment for cirrhosis is directed at symptoms and complications, with abstinence being a requirement.
- A special acknowledgement for the valuable contributions of Marcus A. Rothschild, MD., editor of Alcohol Clinical and Experimental Research, to the development of this Alcohol Alert, without his work, this report would not be available for you to read. (The information in this section is only part of the report given in this Alcohol Alert).

Alcoholism, what is it?

I would like to thank the National Institute on Alcohol Abuse and Alcoholism (NIAAA) for the information found in this section; without their hard work in research, this section would not be available to you the read.

- Alcoholism is a widespread problem.
- Moderate alcohol use- up to 2 drinks per day for men and 1 drink per day for women. A standard drink is one 12-ounce bottle of beer or wine cooler, one 5-ounce glass of wine, or 1.5 ounces of 80-proof distilled spirits is not harmful for most adults.
- Currently, nearly 14 million Americans- 1 in every 13 adults- abuse alcohol or are alcoholics.
- Several million more adults engage in risky drinking patterns that could lead to alcohol problems.
- Approximately 53% of men and women in the United States report that one or more of their close relatives have a drinking problem.
- Heavy drinking can increase the risk of certain cancers, especially those of the liver, esophagus, throat, and larynx.
- In purely economic terms, alcohol problems cost society about $100 billion per year.

Alcoholism, which is also known as "alcohol dependence syndrome" is a disease that is characterized by the following elements:

- Craving: A strong need, or compulsion, to drink.
- Loss of control: The frequent inability to stop drinking once a person has begun.
- Physical dependence: The occurrences of withdraw symptoms, such as nausea, sweating, shaking, and anxiety, when alcohol use is stopped after a period of heavy drinking. These symptoms are usually relieved by drinking alcohol or by taking another sedative drug.
- Tolerance: The need for increasing amounts of alcohol in order to get "high".

Alcoholism has little to do with what kind of alcohol one drinks, how long one has drinking, or even exactly how much alcohol one consumes. But it has a great deal to do with a person's uncontrollable need for alcohol. This description of alcoholism helps us understand why most alcoholics can't just use a little willpower to stop drinking. He or she is frequently in the grip of a powerful craving for alcohol, a need that can feel as strong as the need for food or water.

- Some people are able to recover without help, the majority of alcoholic individuals need outside assistances to recover from their disease.
- Recent research supported by NIAAA has demonstrated that for many people, a vulnerability to alcoholism is inherited.
- It is also very important to recognize that aspects of a person's environment, such as peer influences and the availability of alcohol, also are significant influences. Both inherited and environmental influences are called "risk factors". But risk is not destiny. Just because alcoholism tends to run in families doesn't mean that a child of an alcoholic parent will automatically develop alcoholism.

What is Alcohol Abuse?

Alcohol abuse differs from alcoholism in that it does not include an extremely strong craving from alcohol, loss of control, or physical dependence. In addition, alcohol abuse is less likely that alcoholism to include tolerance (the need for increasing amounts of alcohol to get "high"). Alcohol abuse is defined as a pattern of drinking that is accompanied by one or more of the following situations within a 12-month period.

- Failure to fulfill major work, school, or home responsibilities.
- Drinking in situations that are physically dangerous, such as while driving a car or operating machinery.
- Recurring alcohol-related legal problems, such as being arrested for driving under the influence of alcohol or for physically hurting someone while drunk.
- Continued drinking despite ongoing relationship problems that are caused or worsened by the effects of alcohol.

While alcohol abuse is basically different from alcoholism, it is important to note that many effects of alcohol abuse are also experienced by alcoholics.

What are the signs of a problem?

How can you tell whether you, or someone close to you, may have a drinking problem? Answering the following four questions can help you find out.

- Have you ever felt you should cut down on your drinking?
- Have people annoyed you by criticizing your drinking?
- Have you ever felt bad or guilty about your drinking?
- Have you ever had a drink first thing in the morning to steady your nerves or to get rid of a hangover?
- One "yes" response suggests a possible problem with alcohol. (In the Alpha Program that I teach, we give three tests to determine if a person has an alcohol problem, they are The National Council on Alcoholism Questionnaire, The Michigan Alcohol Screening Test (MAST), and the AA Questionnaire).

Resources:

- People with no insurance can call the Alpha Program at 410-288-1399. This is NOT a treatment program, however the program does provide the client some help. Dr.

Wright never turns a person away because of finances. The program includes education, alcohol, drug testing, counseling, both group and individual, job placement, and assistances with evaluations for court. This program has been used by the probation department, federal, district, and circuit courts of Maryland. In addition, many attorneys throughout the state have sent clients to the Alpha Program. Dr. Wright is retired from the Baltimore City Police Department. He has worked in the Federal Drunk Driving Unit and also undercover narcotics.

- Al-Anon Family Group Headquarters 1-800-344-2666.
- Alcoholic's Anonymous AA world services 1-212-870-3400.
- National Counsel on Alcoholism and Drug Dependence 1-800 NCA-CALL
- National Institute on Alcohol Abuse and Alcoholism 1-301-443-3860.
- Call your insurance company for information about your policy coverage

Assessing Alcoholism:

I want to thank the National Institute on Alcohol Abuse and Alcoholism for the information found in this report No. 12PH 294 April, 1991. Only parts of this report have been used; and its contents are not to confuse or misguide you the reader.

- The goal of assessment is to determine person characteristics that can influence the treatment of a patient's alcohol problem. Once a person has been referred for alcohol treatment, clinicians use assessment techniques to characterize the problem and plan treatment.
- An assessment comprises at least four important tasks: 1. to aid in the formal diagnosis of the patient's alcohol problem; 2. to establish the severity of the alcohol problem; 3. to guide treatment planning; and 4. to define a baseline of the patient's status, to which his or her future conditions can be compared.
- Assessment is an on going, interactive process, used to

164

evaluate a patient's progress and adjust treatment.

- Questions answered by assessment include the following; Can withdraw be accomplished without medication? Is outpatient treatment appropriate? If inpatient treatment is desirable, should the setting be psychiatric or alcohol-specific in nature? What would be an appropriate mix of choices taken from the variety of therapies? How has the patient's status changed during the course of treatment, and what problem areas remain?

- A variety of methods are involved in comprehensive patient assessment, including medical examinations, clinical interviews, and formal instructions (questionnaires or tests). Each has specific strengths, and the approaches complement each other as they address the four goals stated above.

- Most alcoholism assessment instruments are standardized, self-administered questionnaires (or test). These instruments offer comprehensiveness, consistency, ease of administration, and low –cost. (If treatment is needed the major problem is, does the client have insurance or money to pay for treatment. I have found that many clients who are in need of treatment are turned away from program because they lack insurance or funds).

- Assessing Alcoholism – A Commentary by NIAAA Director Enoch Gordis, M.D. Assessment is a valuable tool for alcoholism treatment, and the use of formal assessment instruments as a standard part of all alcoholism treatment programs is recommended. Although formal assessment cannot replace an experienced clinicians judgment, standardized tests and questionnaires can supply clinical wisdom in important ways. For example, an assessment instrument can provide important baseline data for measuring individual patient progress, can aid in making patient / treatment-match decisions, or, in the press of a busy day, can help prevent clinical staff from omitting things of importance at intake. Even programs in which only one mix of treatment is offered can use formal assessments to high-light aspects of a patient's life that need the most help. Formal assessment also can provide standardized patient outcome data that can be used to justify reimbursement and validate the effectiveness of program components.

- The number of programs that use any type of assessment instrument is low, although, there are many advantages to such use. Many programs are concerned that using an assessment instrument may require extensive staff training or time that should be spent in patient care. However, all competent programs perform some kind of assessment, whether it involves a clinician's initial interview with a patient or the use of a formal assessment instrument. In many cases, a portion of the time currently used to conduct initial patient interviews can be devoted to formal assessment without interfering with patient care. Moreover, the variety of instruments that are now available permits a program to tailor assessments to its individual staff and schedule.

New medications:

Today, NIAAA funds approximately 90% of all alcoholism research in the United States. Studies supported by NIAAA have led to the Food and Drug Administration's approval of the medication, naltrexone (ReVia TM), for the treatment of alcoholism. When used in combination with counseling, this prescription drug lessens the craving for alcohol in many people and helps prevent a return to heavy drinking. Naltrexone is the first medication approved in 45 years to help alcoholics stay sober after they detoxify from alcohol.

The Physicians' Guide to Helping Patients With Alcohol Problems:

This guide was developed by the National Institute on Alcohol Abuse and Alcoholism (NIAAA) in conjunction with an interdisciplinary working group of researchers and health professionals. The clinical recommendations in this guide are based on the findings of more than a decade of research on the health risks associated with alcohol use and on the effectiveness of alcohol screening and intervention methods. NIAAA plans to update this Guide periodically to reflect continuing advances in research.

NIAA would like to acknowledge the contributions of members of the Working Group on Screening and Brief Intervention, including the following: John Allen, PhD.; Peter Anderson, M.D.; Thomas Babor, PhD.; Kendall Bryant, PhD.; David Buschsbaum, M.D.; Jonathan Chick, M.D.; Frances Cotter, M.A., M.P.H.; Michael Fleming, M.D., M.P.H.; Richard K. Fuller, M.D.; Nick Heather, PhD.; Yedy Israel, PhD.; Cherry Lowman, PhD.; William R. Miller, PhD.; Judith Ockene, PhD. and Allen Zweben, D.S.W.

Only part of this guide has been use in this section of my book, if you desire a copy of this guide you may call the NIAAA and request information as to how to obtain your own copy. All credit for this section of the book goes to NIAAA and the dedication to all of the researchers working in this field of alcohol and drugs.

Recommendations to patients for low-risk drinking:
- Advise those patients who currently drink to drink in moderation. Moderation drinking is defined as follows: Men – no more than two drinks per day, woman – no more than one drink per day and 65 and over – no more than one drink per day.
- Advise patients to abstain from alcohol under certain condition; when pregnant or considering pregnancy, when taking a medication that interacts with alcohol, if alcohol dependent and if a contraindicated medical condition is present (e.g. ulcer, liver disease)
- If a patient is a risk for coronary heart disease, discuss the potential benefits and risks of alcohol use.

Screening and brief intervention procedures:
- Ask about alcohol use.
- Assess for alcohol – related problems
- Advise appropriate action (i.e. set a drinking goal, abstain, or obtain alcohol treatment).
- Monitor patient progress

What to do about patients who are not willing to change their drinking behavior:
- Do not be discouraged if the patients are not ready to take action immediately.
- Decisions to change behavior often involve fluctuating motivation and feelings of ambivalence.
- Continued reinforcement is the key to a patient's decision to take action.

Things to remember when seeing your doctor:
- Be honest with him or her.
- Tell them about any pains or fears you may have.
- If you have a drinking problem, a letter of treatment from him or her could help you in court matters.
- Always keep your appointments.
- And always ask questions.

Here are some questions that others have asked about alcohol abuse and alcoholism
- Is alcoholism a disease? The answer is "Yes". Alcoholism is a chronic, and often-progressive disease with symptoms that include a strong need to drink despite negative consequences, such as serious job and health problems.
- Can I get unemployment for alcoholism or drug addiction? "Yes". My son Joshua got his unemployment after he came out of the Hudson Treatment center. Just make sure you have your papers from where you have been for treatment or evidence to show you do have a problem.
- Is Alcoholism inherited? Alcoholism tends to run in families. But that does not mean you will inherit the disease.
- Can alcoholism be cured? "No". Alcoholism is a treatable disease.
- Are there any medications for alcoholism? "Yes". There are two types of medications commonly used to treat alcoholism. The first are tranquilizers called benzodiazepines (e.g., Valium, Librium), which are used only during the first few days of treatment to help patients safely withdraw from alcohol. The second type of med-

ication is used to help the people remain sober is naltrexone (ReVia TM). When used together with counseling, this medication lessens the craving for alcohol in many people. An old medication Antabuse that discourages drinking by causing nausea, vomiting, and other unpleasant physical reactions when alcohol is used.

- Does alcohol treatment work? For some people, "Yes", for others "NO"; like any addiction the fight to stay sober is fought day by day. There are many who will relapse several times before achieving long-term sobriety.

- Does a person have to be an alcoholic to experience problems with alcohol? "No". Even if your not an alcoholic, alcohol can still give you negative results in your life; like not going to school, or taking care of your family responsibilities, legal problems can also occur.

- If I have a problem with alcohol, whom can I talk to? You can talk to your friends or family members; however, if your looking for the truth, be ready for an answer you may not want to hear. Listen to what they say and make a plan to do something about it. You can also call 1-800-662-HELP.

If an alcoholic is unwilling to seek help, is there any way to get him or her into treatment?

- You can't force anyone to go to treatment.
- You must be ready to fight with the system if they have no insurance
- The courts can make a person go to treatment, however, without funds or insurance they are facing another problem in their life.
- You must stop all rescue missions.
- You must stop trying to protect him or her.
- Anger is control and communication is fact.
- Do not argue with the person.
- Be very specific and state what the consequences will be.
- Stick by your plan but be ready to get them help when they say their ready.

- If your family stays together on this issue, you will see strength in numbers.

Stages of intoxication:

0.05 Normal behavior.

0.12 Euphoria

0.09 – 0.25 Excitement

0.18 – 0.30 Confusion

0.25 – 0.40 Stupor

0.35 – 0.50 Coma

0.45 + Death from respiratory arrest

MADD

I want to thank MADD (*Mother's Against Drunk Driving*) for the following reports on alcohol. This organization has been a great help to people who have lost friends, relatives, and co-workers in drunk driving accidents.

"Per Se" vs. "Presumptive"

"Illegal per se" means that the operation of a vehicle by a person with a BAL at above a legally defined numerical threshold (e.g., 0.08) constitutes an offense of impaired driving in and of itself. Laws of this type have been proven to have an impact in reducing driver involvement in fatal crashes.

"Presumptive" laws state that a BAC between the numerical threshold and the per se level may be considered, along with competent facts, in determining whether a person was under the influence of alcohol; however, the presumption is rebuttable.

.08 Means Dangerous Impairment:

- An average 170 – pound man must have more than four drinks in one hour on an empty stomach to reach a .08 percent blood alcohol concentration (BAC) level. A 137 – pound woman would reach .08 BAC after about three drinks in an hour on an empty stomach (National Highway Traffic Safety Administration) a level that exceeds what is commonly accepted as social drinking.
- Regardless of how much alcohol is takes to get to this level, at .08 BAC any driver is a dangerous threat on the road. .08 BAC is the level ay which the fatal crash risk

significantly increases and virtually everyone is seriously impaired, affecting all of the basic critical driving skills including; braking, steering, lane changing, judgment, and response time (NHTSA).

- The risk of a driver being killed in a crash at .08 BAC is at least 11 times that of drivers without alcohol in their system. At .10 BAC the risk is at least 29 times higher (Zador).
- More than 20 percent of alcohol – related traffic deaths involve BAC levels below .10 percent (NHTSA).

.08 Saves Lives

- If every state passed a .08 BAC law, about 500 lives could be saved each year. (Hingson, et al)
- .08 BAC is a proven effective measure to reduce alcohol – related traffic deaths. Studied have shown a 6 to 8 percent reduction in alcohol – related traffic deaths in states following the passing of .08 BAC (MADD).
- Maryland is one of 47 states along with the District of Columbia to have a .08 BAC per se law.
- The BAC level is .08 in Canada, Austria, Great Britain, and Switzerland.
- 72% of Americans support lowering the drunk driving limit to .08 as an initiative to reduce drunk driving. (Independent Gallup Survey sponsored by MADD and General Motors).
- With the help of MADD, .08 became federal law in October 2000, requiring states to pass a .08 BAC per se law by October 1, 2003 or face the withholding of 2% of their federal highway construction funds. States without the law by this date will lose an additional 2% of highway funds each year until 2006. Passing the law before October 1, 2007 allows the return of withheld funds to those states that did not pass the law before October 1, 2003.

Did you know...?

- In 2000, alcohol – related crashes accounted for an estimated 18% of the $103 BILLION in U.S. auto insurance payments. Reducing alcohol – related crashes by 10%

would save $1.8 BILLION in claims payments and loss adjustment expenses. (Taylor, Miller, and Cox, 2002)

- In 2000, the average alcohol – related fatality in the United States costs #3.5 MILLION. The estimated cost per injured survivor was $99,000. (Taylor, Miller and Cox, 2002)
- In 2002, the societal costs of alcohol – related crashes in the United States averaged $1.00 per drink consumed. People other than the drinking driver paid $0.60 per drink. Taylor, Miller and Cox. 2002)
- Alcohol – related crashes in the United States cost the public an estimated $114.3 BILLION in 2000, including $51.1 BILLION in monetary costs and estimated $63.2 BILLION in quality of life losses. People other than the drinking driver paid $71.6 BILLION of the alcohol – related crash bill, which is 63% of the total coast of crashes. (Taylor, Miller, and Cox, 2002)
- The total cost attributable to consequences of under-age drinking was more the $53 BILLION per year in 1998. (Pacific Institute for Research and Evaluation, 1999)
- The risk of a driver who has one or more DWI convictions becoming involved in a fatal crash is 1.4 times the risk of a driver with no DWI conviction. (NHTSA, 2000)
- About 1/3 of all drivers arrested or convicted of driving while intoxicated or driving under the influence of alcohol are repeat offenders. (Fell, 1995)
- Drunk driving is the nation's most frequently committed violent crime. (MADD, 1996)
- Drunk driving deaths have reached a plateau. Preliminary alcohol – related traffic fatality statistics show that 16,652 people died on the roadways in 2001. (NHTSA, 2002)
- An estimated 513,000 people are injured in alcohol – related crashes each year, an average of 59 people per hour or approximately 1 person every minute. (NHTSA, 2002)

- An estimated 3 of every 10 Americans will be involved in an alcohol – related traffic crash at some time in their lives. (NHTSA, 2000)
- Americans rank drunk driving as their # 1 highway safety concern. (Allstate – MADD survey, 1997)
- Preliminary research for 2000 shows that alcohol – related crashes cost the public an estimated $114 BILLION annually.
- Approximately 1.5 MILLION drivers were arrested in 1999 for driving under the influence of alcohol or narcotics. This is an arrest rate of 1 for every 121 licensed drivers in the United States. (NHTSA, 2000)
- At BAC's as low as 0.02 percent, alcohol affects driving ability and crash likelihood. The probability of a crash begins to increase significantly at 0.05 percent BAC and climbs rapidly after about 0.08 percent. (Zador, Krawchuk, and Voas, 2000)
- The results of nearly 300 studies reviewed have shown that, at .08 BAC, virtually all drivers are impaired, which includes critical driving task such as divided attention, complex reaction time, steering, lane change, and judgment. (NHTSA, 2003)
- In 2002, 35% of all traffic fatalities occurred in crashes in which at least one driver or non-occupant had a BAC of .08 or greater. (NHTSA, 2003)
- Over four out of five (83% persons of driving age have heard of blood alcohol concentration (BAC) levels, but only 27% can correctly identify the legal BAC limit for their state. (Gallup Organization, 2003)
- For driver's age 35 and older with BAC's at or above 0.15 percent on weekend nights, the likelihood of being killed in a single – vehicle crash is more than 380 times higher than it is for non-drinking drivers. (Zador, Krawchuk, and Voas, 2000)
- The risk of a driver being killed in a crash at .08 BAC is at least 11 times that of drivers without alcohol in their

system. At .10 BAC the risk is at least 29 times higher. (Zador, Krawchuk and Voas, 2000)

- 40% of people convicted of violent victimization (sexual assault, robbery, homicide, aggravated assault, and simple assault) and 25% of the victims had been drinking at the times of the event. (Bureau of Justice Statistics, 1998)
- The available evidence suggests that adolescents are more vulnerable that adults to the effects of alcohol on learning and memory. (White, 2001)
- Alcohol affects all parts of the brain, which also affects the heart rate, coordination, speech, and destruction of brain cells. (Narcotic Educational Foundation of America, 2002)
- The brain does not finish developing until a person is around 20 years old, and one of the last regions to mature is intimately involved with the ability to plan and make complex judgments. (Kuhn, Swartzwelder, and Wilson, 1998)
- Alcohol may encourage aggression by disrupting normal brain mechanisms that normally restrain impulsive behavior such as aggression. (Hingson et al. October 2001)
- Heavy drinking over the years may result in serious mental disorders or permanent irreversible damage to the brain or peripheral nervous system. (Narcotic Educational Foundation of America, 2002)

Holiday Statistics 2002

New Years Eve 118 fatalities, 45 were alcohol related

New Years Day 165 fatalities, 94 alcohol related

Super Bowl Sunday 147 fatalities, 86 alcohol related

St. Patrick's Day 158 fatalities, 72 alcohol related

Memorial Day from 6:00PM 5/24/02 – 5:59AM 5/28/02 491 fatalities, 237 alcohol related

4th July from 6:00PM 7/3/02 – 5:59AM 7/5/02 683 fatalities, 330 were alcohol related

Labor Day 6:00PM 8/30/02 – 5:59AM 9/03/02 541 fatalities, 300 were alcohol related

Halloween 268 fatalities, 109 were alcohol related

Thanksgiving 6:00PM 11/27/02 – 5:59 AM 12/02/02 543 fatalities, 255 alcohol related

Christmas 6 PM 12/24/02-12/31/02 130 fatalities, 68 were alcohol related

New Years Eve 2002 there were 123 fatalities, 57 were alcohol related

Between Thanksgiving and New Years there were 4,019 fatalities, 1,561 were alcohol related.

You can't argue with the facts:

Back in the late 1960's and early 70's a number of states lowered their drinking age from 21 to 18. In many of these states, research documented a significant increase in highway deaths of the teens affected by these laws. So in the early 1980's a movement began to raise the drinking age back to 21. After the law changed back to 21, many of these states were monitored to check the difference in highway fatalities. Research found that teenage deaths in fatal car crashes dropped considerably, in some cases up to 28%, when the laws were moved back to 21. Like it or not, it is clear that more young people were killed on the highway when the drinking age was 18.

News around the United States:

A growing number of companies are adding drunk-driving injuries to the list of exclusions in their health plans, including Chief Auto Parts Inc., Monfort Inc., and Electronic Data Systems Corp. Companies that won't cover drunk-driving injuries are often self-insured. Source of information, Wall Street Journal Abstracts; WSAB Copyright, 1995 Page B; 1:3. (I have a student who was arrested for DUI and was advised by his insurance company they do not pay for treatment in DUI cases this information was provided to him in March 2004).

Sunday, December 27, 1997 Page A-18 Patricia Jacobus, Chronicle staff writer reports, South San Francisco detectives are investigating the death of a 15-year-old boy who may have drunk himself to death at a family Christmas Eve Party, police said, Ruben Castro drank beer, wine, champagne, and hard liquor in excess despite steady warnings from the 30 or so people at the party held by Castro's aunt and uncle.

Drunk driver gets 137 years for 9 crash victims; Wednesday, July 17, 1996 Associated Press reports, a drunk driver got nine prison terms for the nine lives lost in a flaming freeway accident on Father's Day 1995. The total sentence for Teodolo Bermudes was 137 years, eight months, without the chance of parole. "When I first learned the details of this case, I was heartsick over it," Superior Court Judge J. Thompson Hanks said when handing down the sentence Monday. "He killed a whole family, it's beyond tragic." Bermudes was convicted last month on nine counts of second-degree murder for causing a wreck on Highway 60 near the junction with Interstate 10 outside Beaumont.

May 8, 1997, Winston-Salem North Carolina: "Drunk driver is not given the death penalty in first degree murder conviction". A jury has spared the life of Thomas Richard Jones on Tuesday in a landmark First Degree Murder Convection for Drunk & Drugged driving crash that took the life of two 19-year old students and injured four others. He was given life in prison without the possibility of parole. The jury of six men and six women took one hour to decide whether this would also be the first death penalty case for drunk driving fatal crash. They decided that there was not sufficient reason to kill him, and the family of the victims said that they didn't want the death penalty as well. They wanted him to suffer in prison. 2nd degree murder convictions have been common in America for anyone with a prior conviction for drunk driving, in Jones's case he had two priors. Julie Hansen, of Rockville, Maryland was one of the victims.

Teen Dies after taking painkiller-aspirin mix, Friday, July 12, 1996 page 2B San Jose Mercury News by Katherine Conrad, Mercury staff writer reports, a 16-year old Mountain View boy died early Thursday morning after swallowing a toxic mix of at least six painkillers, 10 aspirins, and then washing them down with beer. Almost immediately, he fell into a coma for 11 days, according to Mountain View police Lt. Patrick Langner. The teen's friends said he took drugs after complaining of a headache and back pain June 29. After swallowing the deadly mixture, he said he felt ill and went to the bathroom. There he began convulsing and then turned blue. His friends called 911 and began administering CPR, but the boy never regained consciousness.

Driver gets 16 years in baby's death, Oct. 23 1996, Associated press – Corpus Christi, Texas. A drunk driver got 16 years in prison yesterday for manslaughter in the death of a baby who was delivered prematurely after an auto accident. The case is one of the first in Texas to test whether a person can be held criminally liable for harming a fetus. Because it touched on the question of when life begins, both sides of the abortion debate closely watched it. It took only an hour for the jury to convict Frank Cuellar, 50, of intoxication manslaughter and six hours to decide on a sentence. Jeannie Coronado, the mother was 7 1/2 months pregnant, the child name was Krystal Zuniga.

Henry K. Lee, Chronicle staff writer reports, A former Alameda County senior deputy district attorney who has been convicted four times for drunken driving was arrested again early yesterday in Berkeley after police found him inside his car on top of a street median, authorities said. Attorney Darryl Billups, 48, who has a private practice in San Pablo, was taken into custody about 2:50 a.m. after failing a field sobriety. Billups was on a $31,000 bail on suspicion of felony drunken driving with a revoked license. Mr. Billups alcohol-blood level was .22.

The San Francisco Chronicle reported on December 5, 1995, Page A18; a 27 year-old Oakland man was arrested for drunk driving and other crimes after he allegedly stole a horse from the stables in Golden Gate and caused the animals death by riding it into the path of an oncoming truck

The Associated Press reports, Payne County Associate District Judge Robert Murphy Jr. ordered David Littlesun to visit the grave of Sean Conover, 19, who was a freshman in college for the next eight years. Mr. Littlesun pleaded guilty to first-degree manslaughter and drunk driving charges. Police said that Mr. Littlesun had a blood-alcohol level of .29; Sean Conover's mother Mrs. Mitsuye Conover said in court, "Our lives will never

be the same, I don't think I'll ever have true happiness again"
Sean was her only son.

Evidence needed for a drunk driving case:

Being a retired police officer, I have arrested over 300 DUI and DWI offenders in a one-year period (While working in the Federal Drunk Driving Unit). Evidence in a drunk driving case commonly falls into five categories.

- Driving symptoms like a vehicle straddling the white line on the highway or an erratic driving pattern always calls attention to the police officer. But did you know that high speeds actually require better coordination and quicker judgment.

- Personal behavior and appearance of the person stopped is also an indicator for police officers. If you have blood-shot eyes, slurred speech, flushed face, leaning on your car for supports, or can't follow direction just provided, is part of the evidence he needs for an arrest.

- Field sobriety test; these may include walking, turning, putting your finger to your nose, or reciting the alphabet. The heel to toe test is also part of the field sobriety. Many people arrested for DUI or DWI have problem passing most of these tests.

- Incriminating statements, and it does not make a difference if you make them spontaneously or in response to questioning. When I am asked, "Must you answer the questions a police officer?" My reply, "It depends on the questions", is the officer investigating or interrogating?

- The last type of evidence is the actual chemical test. You have the right in Maryland to take a breath test or blood test. Did you know if a person burps or belches, and then blows into the machine, that the machine could give a false high reading for about 15 minutes? There are many machines on the market; in Maryland the person doing the chemical tests must be certified to operate the machine.

Basic question and answers you need to know:

- Do you have to be drunk to be convicted of drunk driving? No! If you refuse the chemical tests the officer will charge you with the more serious offense. The judge will make the determination whether you were drunk or not. I suggest you always take the chemical test. However, your attorney may suggest that you do not take a chemical test; however, in Maryland if you refuse the chemical test you could lose your driving privileges for up to 120 days.

- What is "drunk driving" in a legal term? Sometimes called driving while intoxicated, DWI, or driving under the influence, DUI, has three general meanings. A. Driving with any amount of alcohol in your system, which causes your physical abilities to be impaired in anyway. B. Driving with a level of alcohol in your system, which amounts to .08 of blood alcohol content. To be guilty of this offense, absolutely no impairment of any or your physical abilities is necessary. You can be the best driver in the world and the safest, but if your BAC is .08 or above you are guilty of a criminal offense. C. Driving with drugs in your system or with a combination of drugs and alcohol, no matter what the amounts of those substances may be, where your physical abilities have become impaired in anyway. If does not matter if the drugs are legal or not, if you are impaired because of taking them, you are guilty of a criminal offense.

- Does the police officer need a reason to stop you? Some officers do what are called car stops; however, legally he or she must have a "reasonable suspicion" based on something unusual that is actually observed about the way a person is driving.

- If I am stopped for an investigation of DUI what should I do? Stay clam and do as the officer tells you. If you have not been drinking you should have no problem answering the officer questions. Never argue with the officer and try and be as cooperative as possible.

- Can the officer search my vehicle if I am arrested? Yes! If you are arrested for DUI or any other offense the officer can do an inventory search of your vehicle. If he finds something in the car that should not be there you may be charged with that also. In addition, the officer can tow your vehicle to an impound lot if he or she feels it is necessary to do so.
- Can I still lose my drivers license if I put the breath machine on my vehicle? Yes! If you have the breath machine put on your vehicle and you have not gone to court for your DUI or DWI, you could still lose your driving privileges if convicted in court for that offense; because the points assets on your driving record for the DUI or DWI will either be a suspension or a revocation.
- How long do the points stay on my driving record? Points stay on your driving record for two years. However, a DUI or DWI conviction will always stay on your driving record even after the points come off.

New Comar guideline for all DUI and DWI offenders:

Every offender who is referred for a DUI or a DWI must have a thorough substance abuse evaluation. The following criteria should be considered in the evaluation to determine if the client is a "Problem Drinker" and needs at least 6 months of Outpatient Treatment.

- Previous alcohol or drug related offenses. Found on driving record or criminal record.
- Prior treatment for substance abuse.
- BAC of .15 or above or positive reading before 12:00PM. Normal work schedule.
- The client refuses the Breathalyzer / blood test.
- Subsequent offense, during the alcohol education period.
- Client is under the influence at the time of their assessment or client shows up to an education class under the influence. (Program must have the capability to test client who they suspect are under the influence).
- Any illicit drug use.

180

- If the client states they have a problem.
- Client is under the age of 21 at the time of arrest.

Justification

Whatever the guidelines, criteria, or assessment instrument used for evaluation and referral the **Final decision** should be based on the evaluator's **knowledge and skills**. No one criteria or guideline should be absolute. However, if the clinician chooses to deviate from these guidelines, the reason should be clearly articulated.

If the assessor determines that the individual is a "Social Drinker", despite meeting one or more of the above criteria, a letter must be sent to ADAA, DWI Coordinator explaining how they arrived at this determination based on their evaluation. A copy of the evaluation must also accompany the letter.

In addition, the clinical director of the program must also review and sign the evaluation. Each program must maintain a list of clients with ID numbers of that evaluation who deviated from the above guidelines so they can be reviewed during site visits.

If the clinician concludes that the client needs a different level, modality, or intensity of treatment, they are obligated to reassess the client and contact the referral source. **The ultimate responsibility for the client lies with the treatment or education program.** The program can choose not to treat the client. The program can offer them other referrals if the client does not want to accept their recommendations.

It is acceptable practice to reassess the client; if at some point before or during the education, the clinician has reason to believe that the client is not a "Problem Drinker". They should included in the contract / agreement to participate that the client signs before entering the relationship.

Clinicians have an ethical obligation when they assess clients. Every evaluator must consider him or herself an agent of the state responsible for making decisions or recommendations that have public safety implications.

- Did you have a proper and thorough evaluation?
- Does your evaluation have public safety implications?
- Did you meet the criteria for being a "Problem Drinker"?
- You have the right to ask for a referral to another program if you do not want to accept the one offered to you.
- Do you have the understanding of the term "final decision"? Remember, it is based on the evaluator's "knowledge and skills".
- However, the setting judge can make a decision for what is best for the client and the public safety. If you are not going to a program because of finances or insurance, WRITE a letter to the judge and ask if he will move you to another program. Many violations after DUI arrest are because a client is not attending his or her required program. Let the judge know about your problems and keep going to your required program. If you stop attending you may find yourself in big trouble with the courts. The following is a copy of a letter you may wish to send to the judge in your case.

To The Honorable Judge

Dear _____ I was in your court on for a DUI offense. My case Number is _____ the date I appeared in your court was _____ of 2004.

I am sending this letter to you because I am having a problem paying for my required treatment program. (Explain your finances at this point). I am requesting permissions to attend (Name the program you wish to attend) because it fits within my budget. I do not have insurance to pay for the program. I am presently assigned to, _____ (Name the program you have been sent to) and I feel that if I remain in this program I will violate my probation, because I can no longer pay for this required treatment. Then sign your letter and mail it. Keep a copy for your records.

Alcohol and Suicide:

The exact nature of alcohol's role in suicide is unclear. Many explanations have been proposed (Murphy et al. 1992,Shaffer 1993, Garvey and Tollefson 1982, Zeichner et. al. 1994, and Young 1992). Nonetheless, a strong association exists between alcohol use and suicide.

- Between 18% and 66% of suicide victims have alcohol in their blood at the time of death (Roizen 1988; Welte et al. 1988, Collier, 1986,Berelman et al. 1985).
- People who drink are twice as likely, and people whose drinking results in trouble at work are six times as likely, as others to commit suicide in the home (Rivara et al. 1997).
- One study suggest that alcohol may be a factor in "impulsive" or "spontaneous", as opposed to "planned" suicides. Alcohol was found to be involved more frequently in suicides in which the victim left no suicide note, had not made a prior suicide attempt, and had no long-standing physical or mental condition to which the suicide could be related.
- A recent study found that states in which more spirits are sold per capita have higher suicide rates, and concluded that a 10% increase in spirits sales would result in a 1.5% or 1.4% (two samples were used) increase in suicide.
- I want to thank ARIV for the information used in this report.

Maryland code / Health – General / Title 8 Alcohol and Drug Abuse Administration Subtitle 5. Alcohol and Drug Abuse – Publicly Intoxicated Individuals, Court ordered Evaluation and Voluntary Treatment / 8-505. Evaluation of criminal defendants.

The information in dark print above is where you can find the codes to health care dealing with alcohol or drug addictions.

The Following are some of the topics you can read-up on, if you have questions call and ask to speak to a director.

- Waiting List Equity Fund section 7-206
- Admission of intoxicated individuals and chronic alcoholics to private and public hospitals section 8-509

- Admission to a facility section 8-502
- Commitment for treatment section 8-507
- Outpatient and aftercare treatment section 8-508
- .11 Special Needs Population – Individuals in need of substance abuse treatment 10.09.65.11
- .02 Provider Qualifications 10.09.37.02
- .10 Benefits – Substance abuse treatment services 10.09.67.10
- Programs section 8-401
- Evaluation of criminal defendants section 8-505

Answers to Test Questions:

1. An alcoholic looks like anyone in your classroom. According to Alcohol Anonymous, a person can be an alcoholic when he or she drinks their life becomes unmanageable.

2. According to the ADAA Health Department, there is no one criteria or guideline that is absolute, the evaluation gives some lead way to the clinician. A treatment program is a place a person will go to if they have problems with alcohol or drug abuse / addiction. Some programs are inpatient, others are outpatient. In this state the law says your legally intoxicated if you have a .08 blood alcohol content or (BAC). An AA meeting, the name is Alcohol Anonymous. They have groups for both men and women, young and old that support each other in a group setting.

3. Yes! Alcoholism is a disease. It starts out slowly and progresses through the years. There are three stages to alcoholism. Early stage, middle stage, and final stage. Some believe it is genetically passed on.

4. A person can drink once a year and be an alcoholic.

5. They are all the same.

6. Most people think a drunk driver is someone that is falling down, swaying, or stumbling. However, in Maryland a .08 is legally intoxicated.

7. Survey shows that about 43% of all DUI and DWI arrest are women and 66% are men.

8. You never mix medication with alcohol. Why? Because you can die from mixing medications with alcohol.

9. Drunk drivers have a pattern of driving to slow, driving too fast, staying in their lane of traffic, driving through stop signs, and going through red lights. These are only a few patterns the drunk driver has.

10. This figure is close but not absolute, on an average we lose about 42,000 each year in traffic accidents; $1/2$ of the fatal are due to the consumption of alcohol.

11. Simple rule to follow is the number 1-2-3 rule. First DUI, if convicted, is a $1,000 fine and 1 year in jail; the second is a $2,000 fine and 2 years in jail; the third is a $3,000 fine and 3 years in jail.

12. This is a personal question. Some people feel that everyone should go to jail and others feel jail is not the answer. I had a student in my class that had 10 alcohol related arrest and killed a child in O.C., Maryland and the state still gave him a driver's license.

13. A friend sent me this information; some say it is close to being correct other have their doubts.

- Australia: The names of drunk drivers are sent to local newspapers, and are printed under the heading, "He's Drunk And in Jail".

- Malaya: The driver is jailed and if he is married his wife is jailed too. Even if she was home with the children.

- Turkey: The drunk driver is taken 20 miles from town and forced to walk back home under escort.

- Norway: The first offense, three week-ins in jail with hard labor; loses of driving privileges for one year. The second offense within a five-year span, you lose your licenses for life.

- Finland and Sweden: Automatic jail for one year and with hard labor.

- Costa Rica: Police will remove the license plates from the vehicle.

- Russia: The license is revoked for life

- France: Three years loss of license, one year in jail, and $1,000 fine.
- England: One-year suspended licenses and a $250.00 fine.
- Poland: You are jailed, given a fine, and forced to attend political lectures.
- Bulgaria: The second conviction results in execution.
- El Salvador: The first offense is your last, execution by firing squad.

14. Alcohol dependency can cause what is called grand-mal-convulsions (these are severe epileptic convulsions). These convulsions are a poisoning effect on the mind; they are difficult to control. Withdraw syndrome could cause death to the person who is experiencing this condition. This is why treatment is some important. A person who is a habitual drinker could have irreversible brain damage.

15. Advertising sells the product. Remember the "Bud Bowl" during the Super Bowl a few years ago. How can we forget that commercial? By the way do you remember the score of the game? See how important advertising is. We remember the product but not the score of the game.

16. People drink for a number of reasons, here are a few reasons people have shared with me over the years. "I am in a bad marriage", "I lost my job", "I went out with my friends", "I have family problems" and "What's the harm in having fun?".

17. A responsible drinker is a person that never drinks and drives.

18. A person is a non-responsible drinker when he or she drinks and drives. You MUST remember you only need a .08 in Maryland to be intoxicated.

19. Let the stats speak for themselves
- 25-30% of violent crime is contributed to alcohol abuse.
- Ten years ago the justice system spent 6.2 billion dollars on alcohol related matters. The cost has gone up considerably in ten years.

- Hundreds of billions of dollars are spent every year in health care because of alcohol abuse.
- In social welfare we spent billions every year on people suffering from alcohol problems.
20. Families suffer along with the problem drinker or alcoholic, here are some things a family goes through because of alcohol abuse.
- Embarrassment
- Making up lies to cover up the problem
- Family fights and arguments
- High medical insurance
- Lack of income
21. We spend billions of taxpayer's dollars every year for alcohol and drug abuse.
22. Billions of dollars are spent in expenditures to the justice system; and victims lose of property every year.
23. If convicted of a DUI or a DWI, the person will have placed on his driving record 8 points or 12 points. This simply means you will have your driving privileges suspended for a period of time or they will be revoked for a period of time. What happens in the courts is only the beginning of a person's problem. You may need to place a breath machine on your vehicle and you may have a restriction placed on your driving privileges.
24. There are a number of myths about just how a person can sober up; a cold shower, hot coffee, or taking an aspirin before you go out are only myths.
25. The BAL is the blood alcohol level and the BAC is the blood alcohol content.
26. There are two tests to determine the BAL or the BAC, one is the blood test and the other is the Breathalyzer.
27. Companies lose billions of dollars every year because employees are dependant on alcohol and drugs.
28. Your cost must include the following; lawyer fees, loss of time from work, tow bill for your vehicle, bail money, fines in court, high rates from your insurance company,

the cost of programs that you must attend after court and fees to the MVA.

29. Fetal alcohol syndrome; the following are some problems that a fetus may have do to the use of alcohol.

- Doctors now agree that the first 12 weeks of pregnancy is the most important time. It is during this time that alcohol intake can cause most of the damage to the fetus. Doctors are now saying, that there should be NO alcohol use during a pregnancy.

- Alcohol can damage the fetus and cause mental retardation.

- If alcohol is used during pregnancy, it is possible for the child to have a growth deficiency.

- Parts of a baby's body that are most effected will be the brain and the development of the eyes.

- Most babies of alcoholic's are born small; they are not usually underweight for their size and length. However, the baby's eyes could be relatively under size.

- The mid-face of the child is small, giving a flat lateral facial contour.

- For doctors the most important concern is the adverse effect of ethanol on the brain growth. The brain tends to be small and mental deficiency of all degrees from mild cases to extreme is found.

- Most children will develop behavior problems along with poor coordination.

- The IQ of the child is also at risk.

30. The chemical formula for alcohol is C_2H_5OH

31. The alcohol we consume is called ethyl alcohol. In chemistry it is called ethanol.

32. Here are a few of the final stages of alcoholism; staying intoxicated for days at a time, seeing or hearing things that are not there.

33. Here are some of the medical effects on the body when a person has been using alcohol heavily; cirrhosis of the liver, neurological disorders, pancreas problems, eye problems, and stomach problems.

34. A person in denial is one who is not admitting they have a problem. For many people that have an alcohol or drug problem it takes years for them to admit it.

35. Hangovers often disappear after early drinking experience. Later, with tolerance and high prolong use of alcohol, hangovers are replaced by alcohol withdraw syndromes. Anxiety, insomnia, and tremors are early signs of alcohol withdraw.

36. Heavy alcohol use will cause inflammation in the lining of the stomach; this will then cause nausea and vomiting. It may also cause upper intestinal bleeding. This could be life threatening

37. The liver is the filtering plant in the body. The job of the liver is to purify the blood. In heavy alcohol use the liver has an increase of fat in the cells. The heavy user of alcohol could have a condition called alcohol hepatitis. This should not be confused with viral or drug induced hepatitis. Also, the heavy user of alcohol may have a condition know as alcoholic cirrhosis.

38. The consequences of alcohol abuse are catastrophic for the abuser, their family, friends, and co-workers. Alcoholism is progressive disorder it effects the entire body. Over a period of time it will take it's toll on everyone who lives with, or associated with, the alcoholic.

39. The brain has many parts, and alcohol will effect the entire brain from speech to body movements.

40. The eyes are effected when a person drinks too much alcohol. To have a clear picture of any object the rays of light must be focused on the retina. This is accomplished by means of the eye lens. This lens is surrounded by muscle that helps bring objects both far and near, into focus. If the muscle is relaxed by alcohol, this causes a distortion of light rays appearing on the retina. The results are interference in the impulses sent to the brain, thus causing a fuzzy picture. The eye has a hard time distinguishing colors when it is effected by alcohol

consumption. Portions of the retina, known as the cones, can make it possible to distinguish between colors. After alcohol use the sensitivity of these cones are decreased, it then becomes difficult to distinguish colors, traffic signals could then become a problem for the person drinking and driving.

41. Alcohol starts in the mouth and travels down into the stomach, then goes into the small intestines and the blood stream and travels to the liver; from there it travels to the brain.

42. Detoxification is a time of sobering up. You may hear people say "someone was in detox", this means the person may be in an in-patient facility. A person that is going through detoxification may need medical attention. Millions go through this on their own with out any problems at all. Remember, a person who is intoxicated may not look or act intoxicated even to the trained eye.

43. Read the chapter on the enabler for this answer.

44. I have found the that Hudson House in Salisbury Maryland to be one of the best inpatient programs around. I have used this program for my son and they did a fine job. You may know of some programs that can be helpful to others. Make a list of them in your notebook.

45. Outpatient programs can be found in your community, you may wish to call the health department and ask for assistance in the outpatient programs. For people who do not have insurance or a lot of money for treatment the Alpha Program located at 1799 Merritt Blvd. in Dundalk Maryland is a faith based program; the program is under the Merritt Park Baptist Church and is NOT a treatment program but runs along the lines of treatment. ALWAYS remember if the person can get into a regular treatment program this is where they will find the most help. However, money and insurance can be the problem.

46. Recovery is when the alcoholic has stopped drinking. They never say they are cured. They're always in recovery. Statements such as "I have been in recovery now for

five years" may be used in alcohol meetings.

47. To name a few alcohol related diseases you may want to have these on your list; cirrhosis of the liver, neurological disorders, cardiovascular disease, and alcohol induced gastritis.

48. A family can do a lot to help the alcohol or drug abuser here is a few to add to your list.

- Be supportive
- Attending meetings with them if asked
- Find locations where meetings are being held.
- Try not to be judgmental
- Remember your dealing with an illness

49. The reasons that some alcoholic's find it hard to change their behavior are, they are still in denial, they have not hit bottom yet, they see no wrong in drinking, and they do not se their life out of control.

50. For many alcoholics, suicide is the answer to their problems this has been called the "termination of the course". Remember about 50% of all fatal accidents are alcohol related. We must also add the fatal fires, the drawings accidents and the hunting accidents. Not all accidents are alcohol related however, many alcoholics feel there is no other way out of their situation.

51. When alcohol is misused the red flag should pop-up. The sooner a problem is confronted, the sooner the abuser is on their way to recovery.

52. The skid row alcoholic; a person who has lost everything and does not care about their appearance, their health, or even a place to live.

53. The Michigan Alcohol Screening test is a test questionnaire about alcohol habits. There are twenty-five question on this test. Each question has a point value with the exception of question number 7. If a person scores 5-9 point on this test they have an 81% probability of being an alcoholic. And if the person scores ten (10) points or more on this test they have a 100% probability of being an alcoholic. In the Alpha Program, we use three tests to make that determination.

191

54. The four stages of on the job signs of alcoholism are:
- Early: late coming back from lunch, leaving the job site early and missing deadlines.
- Middle stages: are borrowing money from co-workers, statements become undependable and there is general deterioration.
- Late middle stages: are failing to return from lunch, hospitalization, increases and there is trouble with the law.
- Late stages: include drinking on the job, being totally undependable, and being generally incompetent.
55. Alcoholism can never be cured. The illness is only in remission. The person who is an alcoholic knows they must take one day at a time.
56. Alcohol was used to clean out cuts, put on gunshot wounds, and used to used to sedate a person before an operation.
57. 12 points are put on your driving record if you are convicted of a DUI.
58. Yes! An inventory search can be made in the vehicle if your are arrested for any crime.
59. A person has the right to ask for a jury trial whenever they face a judge for a criminal offense.
60. The liver cleans the blood and removes all poisons; the liver is know as the filtering plan for the body.

Chapter Nine
A Special Thank You

A Special Thank You For Your Work In Addictions

It's hard to recognize all the people for their work in drug and alcohol research. However, I am sure there is someone I forgot to mention or someone I may have overlooked. I would like to again recognize the many people for the hours they have spent in drug and alcohol research. And thank the many people who are serving the people in Maryland.

The material used in this book comes from the following agencies both private and public; they are in no special order of importance.

- State of Maryland, Department of Health and Mental Hygiene
- Maryland State Police
- U.S. Customs
- D.E.A.
- Baltimore City Police Department
- Special thank you to Baltimore County Narcotics
- Mother's Against Drunk Driver's M.A.D.D.
- All of the newspapers for their stories across the U.S.
- Maryland's Department of Motor Vehicles
- LexisNexis
- Friends in the "Organized Crime Unit"
- Friends in the Probation Department
- Drug Facts Office of National Drug Control Policy
- COMAR
- ONDCP
- National Drug Intelligence Center
- Maryland News Line

- The Criminal Justice System
- Students and Counselors in the Alpha Program
- Maryland Attorneys
- Susan White-Bowden for coming to our class and providing our students with information about suicide.
- And for the Three Angels who work so hard to help others, you know who you are. Thank you for believing in the Alpha Program. I only wish I could give your names, but you ask that "No names be given". Thanks for all of the information and help.
- And a special thank you for the doctors and researchers that I may have missed when using your reports.
- No one was left out of this report deliberately, I am giving all of the credit to you the researchers, doctors, professors, reporters, teachers, law-enforcement officers, probation officers, attorney, and judges for the information found in this book.

SPEAKER INFORMATION

If you would like for Dr. Wright to come to your location and speak to your group please contact him at 410-288-1399.

If you are doing a school project and you are nearby Dr. Wright would be happy to visit your school.

Dr. Wright would also visit your church or any special interest group if you have a need for a speaker.

IF YOU WANT TO START A PROGRAM

If you have a desire to start a program in your school or church, Dr. Wright would be happy to help and your staff get started. You may call him at 410-288-1399 for information.

PROGRAMS AND THE WORK PLACE

If you have a desire to start a program in your work place, Dr. Wright also does consulting for companies. He can set up a program that would include drug and alcohol testing, drug and alcohol evaluations, and education. This program is not a treatment program but an intense education program that could help with productivity in the workplace.

If management knew what to look for in drug and alcohol abuse, it could solve a lot of your companies problems including employee theft.

Dr. Wright is retired from undercover narcotics and was a member of the federal drunk driving unit. He has owned his own company, Cobra Investigation and was a consultant to many business owners.

NEED SOMEONE TO TALK TO?

Dr. Wright will be happy to help you with your drug or alcohol problems.

Dr. R.L.Wright
410-288-1399
410-282-7413 Fax
410-395-0350 Pager